Praise for *Inside the Minds*

"This series provides a practical and focused discussion of the leading issues in law today." – John V. Biernacki, Partner, Jones Day

"*Inside the Minds* draws from the collective experience of the best professionals. The books are informative from an academic, and, more importantly, practical perspective. I highly recommend them." – Keith M. Aurzada, Partner, Bryan Cave LLP

"Aspatore's *Inside the Minds* series provides practical, cutting edge advice from those with insight into the real world challenges that confront businesses in the global economy." – Michael Bednarek, Partner, Shearman & Sterling LLP

"What to read when you want to be in the know—topical, current, practical, and useful information on areas of the law that everyone is talking about." – Erika L. Morabito, Partner, Patton Boggs LLP

"Some of the best insight around from sources in the know" – Donald R. Kirk, Shareholder, Fowler White Boggs PA

"The *Inside the Minds* series provides a unique window into the strategic thinking of key players in business and law." – John M. Sylvester, Partner, K&L Gates LLP

"Comprehensive analysis and strategies you won't find anywhere else." – Stephen C. Stapleton, Of Counsel, Dykema Gossett PLLC

"The *Inside the Minds* series is a real hands-on, practical resource for cutting edge issues." – Trey Monsour, Partner, Haynes and Boone LLP

"A tremendous resource, amalgamating commentary from leading professionals that is presented in a concise, easy to read format." – Alan H. Aronson, Shareholder, Akerman Senterfitt

"Unique and invaluable opportunity to gain insight into the minds of experienced professionals." – Jura C. Zibas, Partner, Lewis Brisbois Bisgaard & Smith LLP

"A refreshing collection of strategic insights, not dreary commonplaces, from some of the best of the profession." – Roger J. Magnuson, Partner, Dorsey & Whitney LLP

"Provides valuable insights by experienced practitioners into practical and theoretical developments in today's ever-changing legal world." – Elizabeth Gray, Partner, Willkie, Farr & Gallagher LLP

"This series provides invaluable insight into the practical experiences of lawyers in the trenches." – Thomas H. Christopher, Partner, Kilpatrick Stockton LLP

ASPATORE

Aspatore Books, a Thomson Reuters business, exclusively publishes C-Level executives and partners from the world's most respected companies and law firms. Each publication provides professionals of all levels with proven business and legal intelligence from industry insiders—direct and unfiltered insight from those who know it best. Aspatore Books is committed to publishing an innovative line of business and legal titles that lay forth principles and offer insights that can have a direct financial impact on the reader's business objectives.

Each chapter in the *Inside the Minds* series offers thought leadership and expert analysis on an industry, profession, or topic, providing a future-oriented perspective and proven strategies for success. Each author has been selected based on their experience and C-Level standing within the business and legal communities. *Inside the Minds* was conceived to give a first-hand look into the leading minds of top business executives and lawyers worldwide, presenting an unprecedented collection of views on various industries and professions.

INSIDE THE MINDS

Child Custody Litigation and Settlements

Leading Lawyers on Establishing Successful Co-Parenting Arrangements and Educating Clients on the Trial Process

ASPATORE

For additional copies or customer service inquiries, please e-mail west.customer.service@thomson.com.

ISBN 978-0-314-29120-2

Mat #41563034

CONTENTS

The Influence of Current Trends in Child Custody on Custody Trial Preparation

William L. Geary

Owner

Law Offices of William L. Geary Co. LPA

ASPATORE

Introduction

This chapter will discuss some of the current trends developing in child custody cases and then discuss preparation for child custody litigation.

General Trends Regarding Language

Certain words that family law practitioners have grown accustomed to using are no longer considered appropriate. For example, even though the Internal Revenue Services (IRS) Code, US Code Bankruptcy provisions, and many decisions deal with "alimony," there has been a movement in many jurisdictions to instead use a term such as "spousal support." Some may think (at least initially) use of the term "spousal support," referring to payment of money to one's former spouse, is a more acceptable concept; however, in reality, the use of the term "spousal support" frequently leads to the situation in which the attorney must explain *"spousal support" simply means "alimony."* Some jurisdictions even discourage the use of the word "alimony" in pleadings, but practitioners may still wish to explain in their documents and pleadings that certain payments are to be characterized as "alimony" for IRS and bankruptcy litigation purposes.

The word "custody" has recently received the same treatment as the word "alimony." Some states and courts have eliminated or attempted to eliminate the usage of the word in statutes and court documents. The word "custody" may be replaced by a phrase such as "allocation of parental rights and responsibilities," and again, the practitioner is left explaining to the client that the term simply means "custody." To be fair, the phrase "allocation of parental rights and responsibilities" indicates more than a custody award, and often involves setting child support obligations, and allocating dependency exemptions, the provision of health insurance, responsibility for the children's uncovered health care bills, transportation responsibilities, and parenting time, as well as many other issues. For the purposes of this chapter, however, the simpler term "custody" refers to the allocation of parental rights and responsibilities.

The Erosion of the "Tender Years" Presumption

In today's courts, the "tender years" presumption seems to be going by the wayside. This could be a result of the shift in viewpoint that has been occurring over the years; the stereotype of the mother or female as the only person capable of providing for young children has been eroded most likely by the reality that fathers, too, can provide for young children.

As the American workforce has changed with the incorporation of women into the workforce, first significantly beginning during World War II and continuing through the fifties and sixties, more families have turned to either the male in the family or an outside provider for help with raising their children. With evolution in the role of the mother as a breadwinner or additional breadwinner in the family, perceptions and presumptions have changed to catch up with reality. Men have taken over not only the care of young children in the American family, but, because of changes in the composition of the workforce, have also taken over many other traditionally female roles in running the households. In the situations where the family employs third-party care providers, the care of young children has been delegated to a source outside of the home. Regardless of whether the father or an outside provider cares for the young children, a "new normal" has been created and society has realized the care of young children can be accomplished by someone other than the mother.

In a situation involving two parents, the presumption is no longer that the father cannot provide for young children. He is given the benefit of the presumption that he is as capable as the mother in the areas of feeding, dressing, nurturing, and providing for the children. Many times this presumption is provided for by statute.

Fathers have endorsed the general population's shift in the presumption perceptions, as well as the shift in the presumptions and perceptions of those who sit as judges, magistrates, and guardians *ad litem* in particular. The reaction has resulted in the formation of various groups for fathers' rights, and the endorsement has resulted in fathers realizing that it is guaranteed that they, too, have the ability to be involved in—or even take over—raising their children.

A Move Toward Shared Parenting: A Child-Oriented Presumption

We must carefully consider any theory that starts with a view of the situation in one parent's favor solely because he or she is the father or the mother. The "tender years" theory started with the assumption (and therefore the presumption, if not foregone conclusion) that the mother was the only parent who could adequately provide for the couple's young children. Time and experience have shown this mother-oriented assumption and presumption were not based upon consideration of the parents' actual abilities. The recent formation of fathers' rights groups and movements has begun creating a father-oriented theory, and, by definition, has given rise to the acceptance of certain father-oriented assumptions and presumptions.

A new and better way to look at all of this may be to create a child-oriented presumption. With that, we could eliminate the competition or challenge of attempting to prove that either the father or mother is able to care for the children, and start with the presumption that a child should have the right to have both parents in his or her life. After all, the child has (hopefully) had each parent in his or her life to some extent before the divorce or custody action began, albeit in differing ways, at different times. This is normal, even in an intact family. One spouse may work more than another, or not at all. One may do all of the cooking or all of the medical appointment scheduling, but the other parent also provides something of value to the family. A desire to keep the child's life as "normal" as possible naturally leads to the issue of shared parenting, or what some jurisdictions call "joint custody" or "joint parenting." This can provide the child with the input of both parents in his or her life. As time passes, the child should also be able to state that he or she lives with the mother *and* father, at different addresses.

Alleviating Client Fears Regarding Shared Parenting

The interesting thing about shared parenting or joint parenting is that children rarely complain about the concept. If someone complains, it is usually one of the parents, and it is usually based on fear or a lack of information. Exploring the possibilities of shared parenting and the fact that it does not mean "no support" or "week-on/week-off" parenting can help with some of the fears a parent may have. Exploring the different ways of assigning responsibilities or decision-making abilities and dispute resolution options can also help alleviate any fear or clarify misinformation.

Contrary to many clients' perceptions, shared or joint parenting does not necessarily mean "week-on/week-off" parenting time. A client must know that in a shared or joint parenting situation, the parties can work out and agree to any schedule they think is best for their children (as long as the court will approve the schedule). For instance, in a jurisdiction where the local rule for parenting time provides that a noncustodial parent could be with the children one evening per week and every other weekend, a shared parenting plan could provide for the same. A shared parenting plan could incorporate the same child support obligations as the court might order if one of the parties were to have sole custody. Likewise, transportation issues, holidays, birthdays, vacations, and other issues can be handled in the same manner in a shared parenting plan as they are if one of the parents has sole custody. Exploring these possibilities with the goal of forming a shared parenting plan can help familiarize the client with what actually constitutes shared parenting, and therefore can help the client adopt that method of settlement.

Shared Parenting as an Ultimate Goal in Divorce or Custody Cases

Even when two parents do not initially agree to shared parenting or joint parenting, there is no reason to abandon that type of arrangement as a final goal in divorce or custody proceedings. As cases progress following filing, there are a number of instances in which the option of shared parenting can be explored during pre-trials, discussions with guardians *ad litem*, and even in the final days and moments before trial—not to mention *during* the trial. The family law attorney must remember that just because a case is in trial does not mean that it will not ultimately settle.

Reviewing the Rules, Case Law, and Statutes Regarding Shared Parenting

Before filing a case and attempting to engage the parents in a shared parenting agreement, it is important for the attorney to review the local rules. First, the attorney must determine if the court has any requirements for attending parenting seminars before it will approve a parenting arrangement and order a parenting schedule. The attorney must also ascertain whether the parties must agree to and file a plan (especially a shared parenting plan) within a certain timeframe before a hearing involving that parenting arrangement. Even if the clients have not reached an agreement, it is important for the attorney to review the applicable rules. Is it necessary to file a proposed plan a certain number of days before the next hearing even if the other side will *not* agree to the plan? What if the other side *will* agree to the plan? Must a guardian approve anything the attorney files before the attorney files it? It is always essential for the attorney to know the rules before approaching a case.

Case law provides the attorney with the appropriate standards to consider even before interviewing a new client in a custody case. The attorney should determine whether the situation is an original action—in which custody has not been decided before—or whether it is a post-decree situation in which custody has been determined, but one or both of the parties is attempting to change some aspect of the prior order.

Finally, it is important for the attorney to be attentive to the standard applicable to the case. Will the attorney be working with a "best interests" standard, a "change of circumstances" standard, or both? This is important information the attorney must ascertain before beginning work on a case. Many statutes provide a number of items a court must consider in allocation of custody. The standards may be different in original custody actions, shared parenting situations, and post-decree situations.

Conducting the Initial Interview in a Custody Case

The initial interview in a case that involves custody issues is most important. The client wants and needs someone to help in a bad situation, so, from the beginning, on all levels, the client must perceive the attorney as caring, confident, and trustworthy—someone the client has chosen to work with him or her. In an initial interview, the potential client has a chance to assess the attorney and the attorney's firm; therefore, it is beneficial to consider what the potential client attempts to accomplish during the interview. In the initial interview, the potential client *should* be looking for an attorney and firm that:

- Know the law;
- Know the judges and court personnel who will be involved in the case;

- Can accurately predict which information likely to be important or unimportant to the trier of fact;
- Know how to intelligently allocate the monetary assets available and avoid exploring information that will lead nowhere;
- Can effectively communicate with the client in terms that are easy to understand, not in technical terms or legalese;
- Actually care about the client and the case; and
- Respond to telephone calls and e-mail messages in a timely manner.

The factors the potential client may actually be looking for in the initial interview may differ from the above list, however. Instead, the client may be looking for an attorney and firm that:

- Do not care about the law and can figuratively "destroy" the other party or help punish the other party;
- Resist everything the other side wants to do or have, just to make the situation miserable for the other party;
- Guarantee results;
- Guarantee how much the case will cost; and
- Can take the case on a flat fee.

If the attorney suspects the potential client expects these characteristics in the attorney and firm, the attorney should act in one of two ways immediately following the initial interview: either the attorney should politely decline to accept the case, or work with the client during the interview to test the situation. It is always wise to ask if the potential client has interviewed or been represented by other attorneys in the past regarding the case or situation at hand. If so, the attorney should ascertain on which points the potential client agreed or disagreed with the other attorneys. Listening to the responses can help the attorney gauge the client's mindset. While anger, feelings of rejection, feelings of betrayal, feelings of powerlessness, and other factors may be affecting the potential new client, the attorney must be able to set boundaries and explain how the firm follows the rules, conducts the practice in a professional manner, and represents clients in an ethical way. It is important for the attorney to let the potential client know representation will not include obstructive actions, personal attacks on the other attorney, unfounded delay of the case, or any other such tactics. The client must understand that much of what the attorney can accomplish in the case depends on the court's perception of the attorney as honest and forthright, or as an obstructionist and conniver who may not be trusted. How the potential client reacts to all of this will help the attorney determine if it is prudent to accept the case.

It is not necessary to close the deal before the client leaves the first interview. Attempting to obtain a retainer on the first meeting may leave the client feeling pressured. The attorney should be confident and invite the client to take the fee agreement home and review it, and then call with any questions.

Gathering Important Client Information

If information is available concerning a case for a potential client, the attorney will likely find it beneficial to review that information first. For example, if the client wants the attorney to handle a post-decree custody change, it is important for the attorney to uncover information the client may not have mentioned, such as any findings of contempt against the client, unpaid guardian fees, or other interesting factors that might affect the attorney's desire to represent the potential client. Even in other situations, it can be beneficial to run the potential client's name through local databases to identify any civil suits, traffic tickets, non-payment of bills, evictions, drunk driving, assaults, or domestic violence. Much of this information can be obtained easily on a computer, or with a quick trip to the courthouse. It is inarguably helpful to be able to consider all of those factors *before* agreeing to represent someone. In a custody case in particular, all or any of those factors are relevant and important to the attorney's strategy.

Avoid Predicting an Outcome or Offering a Cost Estimate

Of course, it is impossible to ever predict the outcome of an untried case, no matter what the facts are—too many variables exist. These may include:

- Facts that are slightly different;
- A different judge or magistrate hearing the case;
- A trier of fact who does not believe the client;
- The applicable law suddenly changing the day before the hearing;
- The best witness now refusing to testify;
- A best witness who cannot be found; and
- The client, who was a stellar potential witness in the office, becoming a completely incompetent witness on the witness stand.

For all of these reasons—and many others—the attorney must let the potential client know from the beginning that no outcome is certain, and the attorney cannot and will not guarantee results.

Additionally, taking a domestic relations case on a flat-fee basis or predicting how much the case will cost can be a dangerous proposition. A housepainter does not offer an estimate without first seeing the home, assessing its condition, knowing the price of materials, and being able to reasonably calculate any repairs, weather problems, and other factors that may affect the project. In a family law case, it is impossible to predict all of the variables that will influence the case: changes in the law, unavailability of witnesses, unplanned continuances, illnesses, and level of cooperation from the other side. Because the variables are numerous and substantial, family law attorneys should never provide the client with an estimate or offer to work on the case for a flat fee. If the attorney offers to work on the case on a flat-fee basis, misjudges the client in the initial interview, and later finds the client completely unwilling to settle or otherwise doing anything possible to drag out the case, the flat-fee situation becomes especially unappealing.

If, after discussing all of the options and variables associated with the case, the client does not want to work with an attorney who refuses to conduct himself or herself in the manner the client desires, then the client can go elsewhere, and the attorney can breathe a sigh of relief. Life will be much easier than if the client had stayed. Alternatively, if the attorney and client can reach a genuine understanding of how they both should act to professionally and ethically conduct the client's case, the attorney can take the next step by discussing communication and fees.

Preventing Communication and Fee Problems

Most attorneys do not practice in all areas of the law; however, it is common for people to approach them at parties or gatherings with a variety of legal problems. It is important for an attorney to tell those people he or she does not know everything—people even appreciate hearing the attorney admit that he or she is not omniscient. Even when faced with questions within the applicable practice area, attorneys are still likely to encounter questions to which they do not know the answer. In such cases, it is best to admit uncertainty and offer to find the answer.

Good communication must start at the beginning of the attorney-client relationship. Interestingly, in most malpractice cases, instead of complaining first about the actual act of malpractice, former clients usually complain first about the attorney never returning their calls. Family law practitioners should take this as a warning, and avoid letting a client feel unimportant and neglected. Clients do not call or email their attorneys just for the fun of spending money.

Essential Components of a Fee Agreement

When accepting a case, it is critical to obtain a signed fee agreement and a retainer before beginning work. From the beginning, the attorney should be direct in explaining the fee agreement, and inviting the potential client to review it, ask questions, and even show it to family members or a third party for a second opinion. If the attorney bills in tenths of hours, the attorney must include this in the fee agreement and explain to the client that a tenth means "six minutes." If the attorney bills a minimum of one tenth of an hour, the client must understand that means he or she will be billed for even one minute the attorney spends working on the case. Likewise, the attorney must clearly notify the client if he or she bills for telephone calls.

In addition to making sure the fee agreement covers what the jurisdiction ethically requires, the attorney must ensure it provides a source of funds that enable the attorney to complete the case. An evergreen fee agreement, with an original deposit or retainer amount and the ability to withdraw monthly expenditures for fees and costs, is one way of ensuring the attorney has access to the necessary resources. If the attorney requires an evergreen fee agreement, it is important to communicate the details of the agreement with the client, including whether the amount of the original deposit will increase or decrease at any time, such as if a dissolution turns into a divorce action or the case looks as though it is going to trial. The attorney should tell the client that the attorney intends to *absolutely* adhere to the evergreen requirements—after all, what kind of attorney does not adhere to his or her own contracts and standards? The attorney should act professionally and be at ease with the fee agreement.

Regardless of the fee agreement's requirements, the attorney must monitor whether the client is complying with the agreement. It is *the attorney's* fault if he or she suddenly finds, days away from trial, that there are insufficient funds in the trust account. At that point, the attorney is probably working for free. If the client requests any change in the fee agreement, the attorney must be extremely careful not to set a precedent with the potential client.

Formulating a Custody Case

After accepting a case, the attorney must formulate a plan. At this point, the attorney should know at least the client's version of the facts, and know what the statutes and rules require. The attorney also should have looked at public records regarding the case and the client. With this knowledge, the attorney can determine where to take the case.

Using the Opposition's Map

Regardless of whether the attorney has a motion to present, if the case necessitates responding to a motion filed by the other side, then the attorney has a map of the opposition's strategy. This map is either composed of a motion, or possibly even a motion and supporting affidavits or exhibits. Regardless of whether the theories set forth in the motion are true, the attorney knows where the other side is heading. Presumably, the testimony and exhibits will follow the outline set forth in the motion and any affidavit supporting the other side's motion.

If there is a motion already at issue when the attorney takes a case, the first steps of preparation should include breaking down the elements of that motion, outlining them, and asking the client a series of questions, including whether the claim is true or false, and why; if the claim is false, if there is any evidence to prove it is false; and if there is evidence, what form it is in (such as documents or witnesses)? The attorney can then determine how to obtain such evidence and get it admitted at trial.

Creating a Map

When creating a motion, the attorney must identify the problem area and issues, as well as the relevant statutes and case law. Only then can the attorney begin to outline the case plan. In outlining the case plan, the attorney must decide:

- Which motions to file;
- Which statutory elements or facts/theories to include in those motions;
- When to file the motions; and
- The best way to prove, at trial, the elements of those motions. This includes identifying the evidence that exists to support the attorney's theories, and how to get the physical evidence admitted at trial.

Including the Best Evidence in the Case: The Temporary Orders Stage

In any case of any kind enough cannot be said about the importance of preparation for trial. Early preparation is particularly vital, as it helps identify the issues and also allows the attorney to determine if it will be possible to obtain the witnesses and evidence necessary to the case. Additionally, nothing is more likely to cause a settlement than the immediate ability to go to trial.

Obviously, in any case, the attorney must determine how much of the actual evidence to reveal to the other side at any given time. If the attorney is filing an action in which the court will issue temporary orders regarding parenting, such as in a divorce action, the attorney should give the custody part of the case the most attention up front. Temporary orders often set the tone for the remainder of the case and other decisions related to the case.

Temporary Orders Granted After Oral Hearing

If the court will issue temporary orders in an oral hearing, the attorney must have ready all witnesses and exhibits by the time the hearing is scheduled. It is important to identify any time limits dictating how long the hearing can last or how long each party has for his or her presentation. The attorney should determine which witnesses to use in which order, and, if possible, rehearse with the witnesses to time the presentation—keeping in mind that nothing ever works out as timed in the actual presentation. A good practice is to leave oral examination of the client until last, so that he or she can hear all of the other witnesses and any cross-examination.

Temporary Orders Granted After Submission of Affidavits

If the court will decide temporary orders upon submission of affidavits, the attorney should refrain from using a form affidavit every witness has signed, as that is unlikely to impress the magistrate or judge. Instead, the attorney should seek interesting witnesses. Of course, the client's best friend and parents are likely to want to help, and there is nothing wrong with that, but other people may help, too. Teachers, neighbors, health care employees, and even ex-spouses (but only the ones who have custody of their own children) may help tell compelling stories that keep the judge or magistrate interested in the case.

Preparing Witnesses to Testify

Witness testimony, whether oral or through affidavits, should tell a story. Every trier of fact who picks up an affidavit or swears in a witness in a custody matter already knows the witnesses will say it is in the children's best interest to be with the client because of the relationship the children have with the client, the client's involvement in the children's lives, and the fact that the client is the one making dinner, scheduling doctors' appointments, and helping with homework. Form affidavits or questions merely list these elements, and each witness can testify in the same manner; however, telling a story makes each witness' testimony more interesting. This may be accomplished by having the witnesses talk about things such as:

- How long the witness has known the children and parents;
- The nature of the witness' involvement with the parents (as a neighbor, health care provider, or co-worker, or otherwise);
- The nature of the witness' involvement with the children (as a grandparent, teacher, or neighbor, or otherwise);
- The witness' relationship with the children—for example, the children confide in the witness, or sometimes reside with the witness; and
- Any particular reasons the witness thinks custody should go one way or another.

Some of the best information might come from neighbors, especially if the children spend large amounts of time at the neighbors' homes or if the neighbors have been closely involved with the family during neighborhood events, backyard barbeques, or even vacations, where they have been able to observe the family dynamics. If possible, the witnesses should stress the client's strengths and the relationships the children have with the client instead of attacking the other parent, unless there are factual situations that absolutely must be discussed.

Creating an Affidavit or Testimony from a Witness' Letter

It is often best for the client to make first contact with witnesses, whether they are friends and family, or even teachers or health care providers. Many of these people probably already have some knowledge that a custody situation is developing. In general, people do not enjoy being contacted by attorneys asking questions or requesting their assistance by potentially participating in a case. If the client can be the person who involves the witness in the process, the case is likely to go more smoothly.

The client can begin by asking the witnesses to write email messages or letters to the attorney. Talking with a witness and listening to his or her opinion of the situation may help shape the case, but having a witness actually take the time to establish a position in favor of the client—and put that position in writing—helps vest the witness in the case and its outcome. Once the witness has created and sent out a letter, he or she will want to know what happens as a result of that letter.

The attorney can provide the client with a list of factors the witnesses should consider when writing the email message or letter. This list should be something the client can also study and think about as he or she prepares for the case; hopefully, it will aid the client in organizing thoughts and developing a sense of what the attorney is looking for in the case. The attorney must design the list to consider the applicable statutes and case law, and amend the list to fit the situation in the case at hand. A sample letter is included in Appendix A of this chapter.

Once a potential witness writes an email message or letter for the client, the attorney has the ability to assess the witness' knowledge, biases, and willingness to make a statement regarding custody. If the attorney decides to use the witness, his or her statement can help guide preparation for testimony at trial or in affidavits. If the attorney is not doing hearing by affidavits, then it is important to talk with the witness, at least on the telephone, early in the case to get a sense of his or her demeanor, personality, manner of speaking, bias, and approach to the situation. This is also true if the attorney is doing a hearing on affidavits only, and there is a chance the witness must make a live appearance later in the case.

Hopefully, the witness' letters do not even remotely resemble something an attorney would write, but these letters should tell a story and cover some, if not all, of the necessary elements to the case. In some cases, it might be necessary to ask a witness to rewrite the letter and omit hearsay statements. In most cases, however, the attorney can immediately, word for word, turn these letters into affidavits. If that is the case and the letters are legible, if the court will accept them, the attorney might consider using the letters themselves instead of retyping them. The attorney should create an affidavit letter coversheet with the case caption and affidavit language for the witness—essentially stating the letter the witness wrote is sworn to as the truth. The attorney may then either deliver the form to the witness directly or through the client, with instructions to print out the form—thus creating an original copy for the witness to attach to a copy of his or her letter, sign, have notarized, and mail back for filing. In this manner, the attorney can obtain a personalized witness affidavit without inconveniencing the witness with trips to the law firm, and without the expense of creating a finalized typed affidavit for the witness during an interview. A sample form is included in Appendix B of this chapter.

Preparing for a Trial

Trial preparation should begin at the outset of the case. Most family law practitioners rely on three helpful tools: notes from the initial interview, the pretrial statement, and a trial notebook.

Using Interview Notes

The attorney should store at least a significant portion of the original interview notes electronically. Once these notes are stored, the attorney can also save them under a different name to form the basis for the trial notes. This method preserves the original interview notes, while permitting the attorney to keep ongoing notes as the case progresses. For example, the attorney may add relevant email conversations between the attorney, witnesses, and client, and can even add Microsoft Word versions of portions of pleadings. If the attorney uses Word, it is possible to keep track of certain information in the trial notes by assigning "finders," or codes assigned to different topics, witnesses, exhibits, or research, as he or she enters information. Using finders helps organize notes as the attorney prepares for trial. For example, the attorney might assign the following finders:

- Motions: MX;
- Witnesses: WX;
- Research: RX;
- Topics: 1111.

With these finders, the attorney can then mark up a document—for example, containing a set of questions from an email sent from the client regarding the other party not bringing the children to school on time. The attorney can copy and paste the questions and responses into the trial notes and give the copied material the heading "SCHOOL ATTENDANCE 1111." In another section involving witness testimony and the questions the attorney will ask a particular witness, the attorney should add the witness' name followed by a "WX" to help locate that witness in the notes if the attorney decides to add more questions or uses the computer as a guide at trial.

Creating notes in this manner results in a searchable document. If the attorney ends up with a large number of pages of notes and must add something to any witness' testimony, the attorney can use a CTRL+F command and a navigation window entitled "search document" will appear in the space at the top of the screen. By entering "WX" in that box and then in the boxes below that choosing the box that shows "Browse the results from your current search," the attorney can get a listing of everywhere in the document "WX" occurs—providing a link to the page where the particular witness' testimony begins. Likewise, entering "1111" provides a list of each of the subjects. If, along the way, the attorney entered notes concerning the same subject twice, the attorney will see that subject appearing twice in the list and can combine the notes regarding that subject during editing.

Maintaining a Pretrial Statement

Pretrial statements provide concise lists of important factors that can be used and reused when drafting motions, formulating discovery responses, and preparing trial outlines. Starting the pretrial statement at the beginning of the case, and keeping a running version of that statement, helps the attorney avoid going through the file page-by-page when the pretrial statement is due, and provides the attorney with a constantly available ready reference document for easy access to basic facts when the attorney needs them.

Assembling a Trial Notebook

Exhibits are necessary at trial. Family law practitioners need copies of their own motions, as well as the opposition's. Access to financial exhibits such as tax returns, the affidavits that have been filed in the case, discovery, or third-party records might be necessary. In the course of representing a client, each of these exhibits is likely to come to the attorney at a different time. The attorney has two choices in this regard. The first is to decide to do nothing about these exhibits when they originally arrive, and then review the entire file to see what is there while preparing later for the trial. The second choice is to take these exhibits, one at a time, as they arrive, and put them in a trial notebook. Of course, the attorney is likely to end up with some exhibits not necessary for trial, but it is much easier to have one set of documents in one book and decide to remove something than to have piles of documents, notes, letters, pleadings, and email messages to sort through. To make the process even easier, the attorney may also keep an exhibit list that catalogs every item in the notebook. The items can be rearranged on the list and within the book as the attorney determines the appropriate order of the exhibits.

Practicing for Trial

After the attorney has assembled the necessary witness statements, trial notebooks, notes on the testimony of each witness, marked exhibits, and the theory of the case, the only thing left to do is prepare the client and witnesses for trial. Good preparation consists of having a personal meeting with the client and witnesses and orienting them to what will happen at trial. The attorney must discuss simple issues such as where the courthouse is, how to get there, and what to expect upon arriving. The attorney must also reorient the client or witness to the case's theory, what the case is about, what the trier of fact must consider, what the client's or witness' role is, when the client or witness will testify, what will happen on direct and cross-examination, what hearsay is, how to comport in the courtroom, and how to respond to questions.

After orienting the client or the witness, the attorney should start practicing. At this point, the attorney must be prepared to ask the client or witness the same questions in the same manner in which the attorney will ask them in the courtroom. The attorney must listen carefully to the answers, and make sure the client is answering them adequately and staying on track. Likewise, the attorney should watch for the manner in which the client and witnesses physically comport themselves, including tone and inflection, and be attentive to hearsay. The attorney should explain cross-examination to the client or witness, and emphasize the importance of answering only the questions asked. It is beneficial to cross-examine the client and witnesses or have another member of the firm cross-examine them so they can get a feel for the situation and its dynamics. Finally, the attorney should continue to practice until everything is right.

Conclusion

A custody case's theory is everything. If the attorney can identify the theory and where the case needs to go based on the facts, the statutes, and the case law, he or she will have much more underlying confidence. Although unknown issues may arise or a witness may not do as well as originally anticipated, the attorney can succeed in professionally and competently advocating for the client.

When accepting a case, and throughout the trial process, it is important for the attorney to continually assure the client and witnesses that he or she is fully vested in achieving a satisfactory outcome. The attorney must demonstrate that he or she knows the case, knows what must be done, and knows what the client knows. In this manner, the attorney can quell any fears by letting the client and witnesses know it is not necessary for them to remember everything, and their only task is to tell the truth. They do not need to worry about being nervous in trial because it will feel as if they are having one more conversation with the attorney. The attorney can remind them the attorney will be asking the questions and can prompt them if they forget something or do not answer completely. Finally, the attorney should tell them to trust him or her to do what the attorney was hired to do.

As we have seen, custody-related analysis is subject to trends. The trends may range from the current acceptability of the usage of certain words and phrases through current or changing perceptions and presumptions that reflect the changing relationships we observe between parents and their children. The law and decisions of our courts and magistrates will continue to change with potentially new definitions of the concepts of "parents" and new definitions of the concept of "family" as well as new definitions of "marriage" as time progresses.

Family law practitioners will have to remain attuned to the changes in the law and the changes in approaches to cases, not only in their own jurisdictions but also in other jurisdictions so that they can have an educated and well-based theoretical approach to what is best for the children in their cases, since what is best for the children should be the ultimate issue.

Key Takeaways

- Encourage your client to consider a shared-parenting plan by informing him or her that the schedule, child support, and other child care obligations can be provided for in a similar manner as if that client were to gain sole custody.
- Set boundaries with potential clients and explain that you follow the rules, conduct the practice in a professional manner, and represent clients in an ethical way. It is important for your potential clients to know your representation will not include obstructive actions, personal attacks on the other attorney, unfounded delay of the case, or any other such tactics.
- In addition to making sure the fee agreement covers what the jurisdiction ethically requires, ensure it provides a source of funds that enable you to complete the case, such as an evergreen fee agreement, and clearly communicate the details of the agreement to the client.
- Have your client involve his or her witnesses in the process by asking them to write e-mail messages or letters to you. Talking with a witness and listening to his or her opinion of the situation may help shape the case, but having a witness actually take the time to establish a position in favor of your client—and put that position in writing—helps vest the witness in the case and its outcome.
- Place your exhibits as they arrive in a trial notebook and keep an exhibit list that catalogs every item in the notebook. You can then rearrange the items on the list and within the book as you determine the appropriate order of the exhibits for trial.

William L. Geary, owner of Law Offices of William L. Geary Co. LPA, has been practicing law for thirty-four years in the Columbus, Ohio area. He is admitted to practice in the state of Ohio, the US District Court for the Southern District of Ohio, and also the Supreme Court of the United States. Mr. Geary concentrates his practice in the area of family law and has also engaged in family law mediation, as a mediator, for twenty years.

Mr. Geary is AV-rated by Martindale Hubbell and has been listed, since 1999, in the Bar Register of Preeminent Lawyers. He has also been recognized as one of the Top Lawyers in the central Ohio area by Columbus CEO *magazine and he has been named as one of Ohio's best attorneys by Best Attorneys Online. Mr. Geary has also received the Martindale Hubbell Client Distinction Award. He also is a member of the Hague Convention International Abduction Attorney Network.*

Dedication: *This chapter is dedicated to my father, Eugene J. Geary.*

Creating Successful Child Custody Arrangements: Grooming Clients for Court, Setting Appropriate Client Expectations, and Entering into Alternative Dispute Resolution

James W. Evans

Attorney

Evans Family Law Group

ASPATORE

Introduction

With the advent of social media, society has moved to chronicling their daily lives for everyone to see—including the judge who is looking at pictures from your client's Facebook page of your client doing a keg stand.

As we live in an increasingly unstable and mobile society, due in part to today's global market and economy, custody litigation is no longer focused only on who gets to be the "primary parent" and what child support will be; an increasingly large amount of time and litigation is centered around whether the child should be restricted to a particular city, state, or country, and whether the child needs protection from international abduction.

To be successful in the current context of custody and family law litigation, it is important to set appropriate expectations and prepare the client for the rigors of what a custody battle could entail. Stability, ability to foster an appropriately healthy and positive relationship with the other parent, family and social support, along with the classic issues of mental health, substance or alcohol abuse, or criminal history/family violence, are all issues that need to be considered. Far and above, make sure to discuss these things in particular in the context of a custody matter in which children with special needs are involved, as special consideration must be brought to bear in a circumstance involving special needs children. These kinds of issues are mainstays in today's custody litigation and provide many pitfalls for the unwary practitioner.

However, litigation is not the only required course. In fact, litigation should be considered as only one of many routes to take in achieving your client's custody goals. It is often a source of frustration for me that many of my colleagues get locked into the same thought process over and over and are unable to be creative and think outside of the box. Judges appreciate creative, solution-oriented attorneys who come to court not only prepared for litigation but also offering solutions. While it may seem counterintuitive, oftentimes the most litigious party gets snake bit in the end. So, be creative in your motions and your pre-trial and pre-hearing practice, all the while keeping in mind how to achieve your client's goals.

This chapter will attempt to apprise the practitioner of trends in child custody litigation and give some advice regarding managing/preparing clients for trial or settlement.

Trends in Texas Child Custody Litigation

The Internet

Access to the Internet has changed the practice of family law in many different ways.

The introduction of social media has had a large impact in custody litigation. One would think that as social media is so easily accessible, this would force parents to remain positive and mindful of what they put out for everyone to see and read. However, like a moth drawn to the fire, people cannot help themselves in posting pictures of doing boneheaded things with their children present, or blogging about illegal or ill-advised activities, or starting a twitter war with the other parent. As society has trended toward documenting their daily lives in open forums, Facebook has become a staple of child custody hearings.

I recently dealt with a case where the transfer of an alleged sexually transmitted disease was the issue. The mom was claiming this to be the case where the father threatened her life with cancer. However, when we were able to pull the posts from her Facebook page, she had discussed with many of her friends within Facebook that she did not have any disease or cancer. I have had other situations where a dad wanting to have primary custody or more than standard possession posted pictures of himself in various stages of intoxication, brandishing both photos and video of different kinds of weapons, and racial slurs and highly negative comments about the mother of his children. Needless to say, that hearing did not go well for the dad. Another recent hearing I was involved with was related to the custody of a four-year-old son, where the mom found out about her husband of ten years' affair with his twenty-year-old girlfriend from a Facebook posting.

Needless to say, people just cannot help themselves and social media is a relentless and fertile world of evidence waiting to be harvested against a client by the careful and creative practitioner. Of course, on the other side, the practitioner representing the party with the bad postings should be very careful in how to deal with that evidence to avoid issues related to destruction or modification of evidence and spoliation because, as we all know, it is never really deleted even when it has been "deleted."

Additionally, with the wealth of information available on the Internet, parents have become more self-educated regarding divorce and custody. However, this sometimes works to their detriment. It is one thing to play attorney on television and another to try to play one in real life in a custody situation where the relationship with your children is on the line. The old adage of "garbage in, garbage out" is very apt in describing some of the information available on the Internet. Sometimes a large majority of initial time a practitioner must devote with their client is debunking, or what I like to call "unbundling," their client's misinformation gleaned from urban myths, family and social sources, antiquated social norms, and websites created for the sole purpose to rail against "the system."

Most parents know before they even enter child custody litigation that they will share custodial responsibilities. Most even have some knowledge and basic understanding of custody, conservatorship, and options for possession and access. With the sophisticated client, this gives the creative practitioner the ability to manage a more "nuanced" strategy with the client as they have a firm grasp and understanding of the basic legal fundamentals at stake. This is important, as in my experience and observation, many times these issues turn on nuances when in front of a judge. For example, mom always said it is not *what* you say as much as it is in *how* you say things. Communication styles, not necessarily substance, can have a significant impact in a courtroom.

In these cases, whether parents will be awarded joint custody is typically not the question. Instead, the parties must focus on much more nuanced issues involved with exercising custodial decisions, such as education, medical, mental health issues, extracurricular and summer activities. This is especially true in the situation where a child has special needs.

The idea of a gender bias in favor of the mother is largely gone. Additionally, courts have begun to rely less on the "tender years" presumption that young children should be placed with the mother, and are now focusing on parents' capability to care for their children at any age. The only exception to this general trend is as it applies to newborns, in which case mothers have a distinct advantage. Even so, courts are more willing than they were in the past to grant more visitation time to a father who is capable of caring for his child. In fact, in my observation, a dad who wants, is willing, and is capable of putting time in with their infant child carries a premium with the courts.

This makes sense in an era in which there are more stay-at-home fathers and working mothers. And, in this era, fathers today are much more willing to fight for their parenting rights than they historically were. This has caused a significant erosion of the gender bias and the gender gap has fallen. Likewise, ethnicity and sexual orientation rarely, if ever, factor into a judge's decision regarding custody. Rather, the issue here is how that may, if at all, translate to the children and their best interests.

Age, however, may be an issue if one of the parties is especially young, and the court does not think the parent has attained the necessary maturity level to make important decisions regarding the child's welfare, or has a demonstrated history of making poor decisions, instability, criminal history, or history of alcohol or substance abuse. It is oftentimes in these circumstances the practitioner should talk to the client about being creative and bringing in a parenting coach to assist them and work with them in dealing with a young child. I often find myself having to debunk with my dad clients the idea that a parenting coach is needed—as though it sets a negative precedence that he "needs" or "requires" supervision. The opposite has generally been my experience. If handled correctly, and I cannot emphasize that enough, having a professional parenting coach come and testify can turn the entire case around in the eyes of a judge.

Unfortunately, socioeconomic status can also come into play if a parent does not have enough money to meet the child's financial needs. It is in these situations you have to look for family or social support wherever the client can find it and give the court a source of comfort that this parent can be consistent in exercising time with their child and in a safe and responsible way.

Paternity Fraud

Paternity fraud has become a growing issue in recent custody cases in Texas. It has unfortunately become fairly common years later in the course of a heated argument that a father is "politely" informed that one or more of the children are not even his biologically. Of course, this comes after years of child support and acting as the father, so go figure. Until recently, at least in Texas, a man in that situation was stuck and bound by the prior orders that may have been obtained by fraud in that the mother purposefully did not reveal she had been intimate with another man.

In 2011, the legislature passed a paternity fraud statute that allows for a cause of action for a man who, believing he was a father, did not contest parentage and acknowledged paternity or was adjudicated as the father without a DNA test.[1] If the mother, by acts of misrepresentation, led the man to believe he was the father of the child and therefore failed to contest the parentage of the child, the man can request a court order to conduct DNA testing a number of years later in an effort to terminate his parent-child relationship with the child.[2] A couple of things to note here—first, that voluntary DNA test that the "dad" obtains in secret while the children are with him on summer possession is not admissible in Texas *per se* and absent agreement of the parties. That DNA test has to be done, under these circumstances, pursuant to a court order. Second, the child support the man has already paid is not recoverable. However, if the DNA test reveals the man is not the child's father, the court can effectively terminate that person as a parent and end the man's obligation to support the child.[3]

Attorneys should counsel men to be careful of the legal implications of terminating parentage, however, under these circumstances. The older and more aware the children are, the larger the risk that the relationship with the children could be completely and permanently affected. While the "dad" may no longer be responsible for paying child support, if the client had developed a strong bond with the child he risks being completely cut out of

[1] Tex. Fam. Code Ann. § 161.005(c) (West).
[2] *Id.*
[3] Tex. Fam. Code Ann. § 161.005(i).

the child's life or inalterably changing the relationship between them and affecting that child for many years to come. In those circumstances, it is best to politely maneuver around the lack of paternity, and leverage the mother's fraud to obtain a better outcome for the man, such as equal possession without child support.

Conservatorship and Domestic/Dating/Family Violence

Generally, there is a presumption that parents should be named joint managing conservators of their child unless it would not be in the child's best interest or there is a history or pattern of family violence.[4] Typically, regarding best interest, any or all of the following three issues are present when there is a request that the parents not be named joint managing conservators: (1) drug/alcohol abuse; (2) mental health issues; and/or (3) criminal convictions.

However, it should be noted that a less frequently thought of issue can have a dire effect on a custody case. The Texas Family Code has a special provision regarding domestic/dating/family violence and conservatorship.[5] If a parent has demonstrated a history or pattern of domestic violence, the court is barred from appointing that parent as a joint managing conservator of a child.[6]

There are two elements a court must find to grant a protective order—that family violence has occurred and that family violence is likely to occur in the future.[7] In many cases, practitioners successfully defend against applications for protective orders by showing that family violence is not likely to occur in the future given the specific facts and circumstances of the case. However, practitioners should be extremely weary of focusing solely on the second element as several appellate courts have held that one occurrence of family violence can constitute a pattern or history of domestic abuse, thereby triggering dire consequences regarding conservatorship and possession and access to a child.[8]

---

[4] Tex. Fam. Code Ann. § 153.131 (West).
[5] Tex. Fam. Code Ann. § 153.004(b) (West).
[6] *Id.*
[7] Tex. Fam. Code Ann. § 85.001 (West).
[8] *Alexander v. Rogers*, 247 S.W.3d 757, 762 (Tex. App. 2008).

If it is legitimately questionable that domestic/dating/family violence occurred, a practitioner should do their best to defeat the application for protective order on the first element, or at the very least, make sure that an order denying a protective order does not have a finding in it that family violence occurred but is not likely to occur in the future.

However, sometimes clients come in the door with bad facts that they will have to live with. These types of cases arise where there is obvious evidence that domestic abuse/family violence occurred. Depending on the severity of the allegations, it may be necessary to counsel the client to accept his or her punishment during the first day in court—which is preferable to leaving on a bad note and provides the attorney with the opportunity to utilize an expert to rehabilitate or dismantle those facts later in the case. While the issue of joint custody may be barred statutorily, a history or pattern of domestic abuse/family violence does not necessarily tie the court's hands with regard to possession and access. If the court finds that there is no danger to the child's physical health or emotional welfare and it would be in the child's best interest, a court can fashion any possession and access order it deems appropriate.[9] Best interest and no harm to the child are the themes that should be presented in evidence and argument to the court so that a client, while demoted to a possessory conservator, can still have meaningful frequent contact with the child.

The best approach is often to have the client acknowledge the problem and take responsibility (hopefully without any criminal liability) for his or her actions so the court does not view the client as angry, controlling, or disingenuous. The client must follow the court's recommendations, whether they include individual counseling, drug testing, or anger management. The attorney should counsel the client to quote the lessons the client has learned and how the client is applying those lessons to everyday life in the same terms the court system uses, so the judges can hear their own words fed back to them, at follow-up hearings. This helps in a variety of ways—it builds trust with the judge and also buys time and distance from the original incident or problem.

[9] Tex. Fam. Code Ann. § 153.004(d).

When someone is brought to court under those circumstances, the alleged aggressor is usually defensive. The attorney plays an important role in helping the client move past his or her defensiveness by helping the client realize the court case has little to do with the events that occurred between the parents, but instead centers on the parent's relationship with the child. The attorneys can arrange the custody agreement so the parents never need to see each other or communicate, and their relationship is no longer the issue. The attorney must make the client recognize that the court must understand what kind of parent—not spouse—the client is, and will form its opinion based on the best interests of the child.

Achieving a Successful Joint Custody Arrangement

When creating a joint custody arrangement, it is important to educate the client on the many characteristics that affect the likelihood of the arrangement's success—the first of which is geographic proximity. Shared custody arrangements usually work best when parents live close together, as it facilitates an equal possession schedule. Additionally, communication has a great impact on joint custody. Parents who are able to communicate well can prevent or reduce conflict, especially in front of the children, and can focus on making decisions that are in the children's best interest. Those parents who offer to share responsibility for such tasks as providing transportation to medical appointments or attending parent-teacher conferences, and share information from those activities with the other parent, are more likely to be involved in successful custody arrangements than those who try to seize the opportunity to use their involvement in such tasks as a presumptive litigation factor.

Gathering Information at the Initial Client Meeting

The initial client meeting is the attorney's opportunity to gather most of the important facts to present in the case—both positive and negative. A good litigator understands which information is beneficial, detrimental, or insignificant, and identifies ways to prevent the negative aspects from dismantling the case. It is also an opportunity to develop a rapport and give the client confidence that the attorney will be both effective and trustworthy. Developing clear and open lines of communication facilitates better information exchange, and allows the attorney to reasonably control the client's actions by ensuring the client does not, for example, criticize the other parent through e-mail, hide money, or make secret doctors' appointments.

It is important during the initial meeting to provide the client with an understanding of the actual law, including what terms such as "joint custody" mean, what rights and duties exist, the various possession schedules, and how to conduct exchanges. Many clients have been misinformed either from their own Internet research or from friends/family regarding the actual law. Urban myths abound regarding child custody.

Finally, the attorney should work with the client during the initial meeting to develop a strategy. It is important for the client to understand the strategy from the outset, and understand the steps the attorney will take to meet his or her goals. The attorney must be careful to set clear, realistic expectations for every step of the process without anchoring a client to a particular result—judges can sometimes be unpredictable. If the client has reasonable expectations, however, and follows the attorney's orders and has sufficient resources to pay for the process, it is usually possible to meet the client's goals.

Setting Appropriate Client Expectations

People often fail to recognize the costs and intensity associated with child custody litigation. It can be physically and emotionally exhausting to be at a deposition or testifying for several hours straight. Testifying can be especially demanding at the hands of an aggressive litigator. Clients also fail to recognize or anticipate everything that can go wrong during the process. As a result, the attorney must ensure the strategy is adequate and clear from the outset, and the client is reasonably educated on how the process works and the likely outcome. Clients often approach child custody litigators in hopes of creating an agreement with the other parent, with no idea of how difficult it can be to manage the nuances of manipulating the case and individual circumstances to obtain the right results. Child custody litigators must also teach their clients to be patient and bite their tongues, as the process to accomplish their goals can be lengthy.

It is impossible to form an effective strategy without first identifying the client's goals. The attorney must listen to the client's ideas of a satisfactory outcome, but must help the client determine whether those goals are actually appropriate. A client may believe sole managing conservatorship is necessary due to the other parent's lack of communication, but in reality, that may not be an appropriate goal. Before the attorney can help the client set appropriate goals, the attorney must have a good command of the facts involved with the case. The attorney should, with the client's help, attempt to attack, dismantle, and critique the client's side of the case so the client understands the inherent strengths and weaknesses. The attorney should take the time to explain the court process, how the law will be applied in the case, and a judge's likely action. In this manner, the attorney can temper the client's expectations and obtain a satisfactory outcome.

Preparing the Client for Court

When preparing a client for court and other appearances, it is important to ensure the client understands the facts and strategy related to the case, as well as the expected outcome. As the hearing or trial progresses, it is helpful to prepare the client by walking through the testimony and helping the client rephrase statements in a manner that is honest but also makes a point and does not offend the court—the client must to learn to filter his or her words. Depending on the complexity of the case, it may be beneficial to visit the courtroom, put the client on the witness stand, and conduct a mock cross-examination. The attorney may even record the testimony so the client can hear his or her answers and tone of voice. Rehearsing, followed by the attorney's critique and feedback, can be an especially helpful element in preparing clients for court.

Using Psychological Expert Testimony

Psychological experts can play an extremely significant role in child custody cases by either helping diagnose mental health issues or by determining their severity. They can also determine how difficult a particular issue may be to treat and manage, and whether the issue is likely to translate to child safety issues, or interfere or sabotage the child's emotional development. Often, the expert's recommendations for a treatment plan become incorporated into the court's orders.

Obtaining a child therapist's services is especially important when one parent believes the other has a negative effect on the child's emotional well-being. If the child goes to therapy following visits with the parent and exhibits negative behaviors, the mental health expert's testimony can dramatically affect the case. Alternatively, if the client can work with a therapist to eliminate some mental health problems such as extreme anger, the therapist's testimony can make the difference between being granted zero visitation rights and having extended periods of time with the child.

Challenges Associated with Child Custody Cases

The emotion involved with child custody cases is the biggest challenge associated with this type of litigation. One of the biggest mistakes a parent can make during a custody battle is failing to eliminate the conflict with the ex-spouse. Clients send questionable text messages and post inadvisable statements and pictures on Facebook. Some of the worst mistakes involve refusing to return the child after a visitation or enrolling the child in a new school without telling the other parent. These mistakes are often harmful to the parent's case in the future. Often, over time, removing conflict from text messages, e-mails, and phone conversations leads to the problem organically solving itself, and many times, the other side relaxes as well.

Clients in this area of law have high expectations, but often have limited financial resources to achieve their goals. Additionally, child custody cases can require the client's patience, especially when the child is young. It can be difficult for parents to understand the necessity of planning for the first three years, and then taking more of a wait-and-see approach. Custody cases can resemble a chess game—the client should never negotiate around certain issues, but should instead take various steps and adapt the strategy so one piece moves another.

Navigating Cross-Border Custody Challenges

If the primary parent in a child custody case lives in another country, the attorney must first determine whether the country is a member of the Hague Convention, which means it is possible to enforce possession and custody orders in that country. If the custodial parent is living in a non-member country such as India, China, or Pakistan, the attorney must resort to tricking the parent to bring the child either to the United States or to a member country that will allow the noncustodial parent to enforce custody rights. The attorney should review travel itineraries, school vacations, and the visitation and access schedule for the most extended times.

The threat of international abduction, especially to a non-Hague Convention country, is not an uncommon issue. Courts have at their disposal several measures to deal with such risk. Most commonly courts use passport controls to ensure that a child cannot be taken to another country without the consent of both parents.[10] A little less common, but effective, is that a court can require that a parent put up a bond to help offset the cost of retrieving a child from a foreign country.[11]

Cases Involving Unmarried Mothers with Infants

Many problems arise in cases involving unmarried mothers with infant children. If the couple has not been sharing child-rearing duties, even if the father is perfectly capable of caring for his child, the mother is often concerned the father will not be up to the task. As a result, courts have begun utilizing parenting coaches or consultants, as well as classes the parents can attend together. The purpose of this approach is to provide an environment for people to learn how to communicate their needs regarding their children's care, eliminate false concerns from the custody process, and create an effective parenting plan for the couple.

Cases Involving Purported Abuse

When representing a client where abuse has been perpetrated on the client, it is important to first assess the level of abuse and how real it is. This means determining how and when it happened, as those allegations may work against the client's case in court. For example, I once saw a case in which the mother, who was abused at some point during the relationship, focused on protective orders and domestic violence because the father bit her finger, neglecting to address something more serious that had occurred several years earlier. The judge did not take the mother's claims seriously,

[10] Tex. Fam. Code Ann. § 153.503 (West).
[11] *Id.*

and she lost custody to the father by aggressively relying on a minor incident, even though it technically was abuse.

Cases Involving Substance Abuse/Mental Health Issues

If the case involves substance abuse or mental health issues, the attorney must first triage and assess the level of the difficulty involved by relying on any existing diagnoses. It is critical for the attorney to ensure those issues are under control before entering the courtroom, as the court must determine whether the client can be trusted to successfully manage and navigate the condition, and to be around the child unsupervised for extended periods of time. The client must follow all of the legal firm's standard protocols for that particular condition. When determining those protocols, it can be helpful to consult with an expert qualified in that area. The attorney may employ psychiatrists, or even social workers who are individual counselors, to ensure the client goes to doctor or counseling appointments, manages any medications, and generally has the situation under control. In such situations, clients can often sound caustic and conflictive when they are confronted with the issue, so the attorney should teach the client to communicate in a more appropriate manner.

Using Alternative Dispute Resolution

Generally, when alternative dispute resolution is thought about in the context of family law, mediation is the only alternative dispute resolution method that is discussed. Most advocates are familiar with mediation where a private mediator is hired to help broker a deal, and this is an effective option for people already embroiled in a custody battle. However, a collaborative approach to dispute resolution in child custody cases has gained popularity across the country. Texas has adopted an entire section in its family code specifically addressing the process of collaborative law.

When a client is offered a child custody settlement, the attorneys must look to the future and determine how to lock in long-term gains. If a client does not want to pay child support but is offered a 50/50 possession schedule, for example, it is usually best to lock in that possession schedule with the goal of modifying the child support issues at a later date. When faced with a child custody settlement, it is also important to begin thinking about the mechanics of how the parents will make decisions regarding the child, how they will exchange the child, and how to address the issue of vacations and holidays. Additionally, the attorney must help the client consider any special needs the child may have, and how the parents will delegate the extraneous costs of extracurricular activities, cars, mobile phones, uniforms, and travel needs, as well as tuition and health insurance. If one of the parents has an annual family reunion or makes an annual trip to a certain region, it is also wise to incorporate that into the orders. Of course, it is essential to be as clear as possible regarding these matters.

It is always best to think of all contingencies when settling. It is extremely hard to get out of a settlement agreement that meets the requirements of an informal settlement agreement/mediated settlement agreement. For instance, if you are representing a parent who is in the military and may be deployed at some point, it is best to deal with all possible contingencies including extra possession time when the parent returns from deployment.

Conclusion

During the next year or two, Texas is likely to strike more of a balance in comparing incomes and parents' abilities to meet equally their children's financial needs. Parenting fraud will also continue to be an issue in child custody cases. Additionally, continued advancements in technology will enhance the ability to exercise virtual visitation and allow for virtual conferences between parents and professionals such as teachers, doctors, and mental health providers. This will also allow a noncustodial parent to attend a child's sporting events, for example, in addition to being able to instantly communicate at any time.

General Advice for Family Law Practitioners

Attorneys engaging in child custody litigation must be careful not to get in over their heads. It is important to consult with experienced practitioners, especially if the attorney is new or otherwise inexperienced. It is essential to set client expectations appropriately and set clear goals, and to maintain constant communication with clients. While clients are likely to be emotional, the attorney must have control over the clients so that ultimately they do as the attorney recommends. Otherwise, it becomes impossible to negotiate the case, the associated costs can spiral out of control, and an otherwise decent case may need to be withdrawn.

Beyond having a deep knowledge of the law and the ability to litigate, family law attorneys, especially those who are new to the area, must know how to filter information and understand what is significant and what is not. It is important in limited hearings of temporary orders to know what information will change the case's outcome, and avoid introducing arguments that simply do not matter. This is a nuanced area of law that many traditional family law attorneys do not understand, and the savvy attorney can usually take advantage of their mistakes.

Finally, family law attorneys should not be afraid to be creative, and should ask the court for what they think they need, even if it is not in the family code. Attorneys can style motions and request relief for what they need, especially if case law or a statute supports it. Over time, the attorney can develop a rapport and credibility with the courts, and as a result the courts will trust the attorney's opinions and representations.

Key Takeaways

- Advise your client to eliminate conflict with the ex-spouse/other parent as the court case has little to do with the events that occurred between the parents, but instead centers on the parent's relationship with the child.
- Work with your client during the initial meeting to develop a strategy, explaining the steps you will take to meet the client's goals. Set clear, realistic expectations for every step without anchoring a client to a particular result.
- With the client's help, attempt to attack, dismantle, and critique the client's side of the case so the client understands the inherent strengths and weaknesses of their case. Take the time to explain the court process, how the law will be applied in the case, and a judge's likely action. This will help temper the client's expectations.
- Prepare your client by walking through the testimony and helping the client rephrase statements in a manner that is honest but also makes a point and does not offend the court. Depending on the complexity of

the case, it may be beneficial to visit the courtroom, put the client on the witness stand, and conduct a mock cross-examination.

- When faced with a child custody settlement, begin thinking about the mechanics of how the parents will make decisions regarding the child, how they will exchange the child, how to address the issue of vacations and holidays, and how the parents will divide the extraneous costs of caring for the child. It is essential to be as clear as possible regarding these matters.

James (Jimmy) W. Evans, an attorney with the Evans Family Law Group, has been in practice for sixteen years. Mr. Evans is also a lifetime member of the Texas Academy of Family Law and a lifetime member of the Texas Family Law Foundation. Mr. Evans is a member of the Family Section of the Travis County Bar and the State Bar of Texas and has been admitted to the US District Court for the Western District of Texas. Mr. Evans graduated law school at Texas Wesleyan University in just over two-and-a-half years in 1994. After becoming licensed in May 1995, he worked as an assistant criminal district attorney with the Tarrant County District Attorney's Office. During this time, Mr. Evans prosecuted such crimes as domestic violence, protective orders, family violence, sex crimes against children, and other felony and misdemeanor crimes for nearly five years. During this time, Mr. Evans spent significant time working with children and protecting them against predators. At the District Attorney's office, Mr. Evans was nicknamed "scrapper" for his scrappy litigation style. Thereafter, Mr. Evans worked in commercial litigation with a private firm until becoming a father six years ago. Since that time, Mr. Evans has focused his practice exclusively in the area of family law.

Custody Cases: Fighting for the Best Interest of the Child

Faye Riva Cohen

Owner

Law Office of Faye Riva Cohen PC

Introduction

Litigating a custody case is a vitally important part of the practice of law as it profoundly affects the lives of the youngest and most vulnerable in our society. Over the course of this chapter, we hope to offer helpful insights and unique perspectives into the issues facing custody cases and custody lawyers. Regardless of approach, issue, or aspect of any given custody case, the single most important thing to remember is that a custody case is, ultimately, about what is best for the child(ren) at issue as opposed to any other party, including the parents.

Joint Custody Arrangements

Joint custody arrangements are becoming a more common element of custody orders as courts and practitioners are more aware of the negative impact of divided custody on children, parents, and their respective relationships. The current generation of attorneys and judges who are middle-aged and younger are really the first attorneys of any significant number who, themselves, were raised in families subject to custody orders. They know how custody orders function firsthand, and what it was like as a child to be subjected to them. It is realistic to assume that their life experiences, as well as those of other family members and friends, play a large part in how they approach custody cases now. It is clear that most children miss the involvement of the parent with partial custody and are adversely affected by that absence, and current judges and attorneys remember those feelings when issuing custody orders.

The role of each parent in a child's life is more respected and better understood, especially the role of the father. The increased parenting role of fathers is reflected in the increase of shared custody. Furthermore, the concept of "co-parenting" is gaining prevalence and the benefits of having both parents involved in child rearing are now generally recognized. Traditionally, it was presumed that the mother was the more natural, and therefore more capable, parent. The new Pennsylvania custody statute, which became effective in January 2011, specifically mandates that the genders be treated equally before the court in any custody case. The result of years of custody litigation has resulted in the conclusion that fathers can be, when given the opportunity, just as effective and capable at parenting, as mothers. This realization has led to the courts granting fathers shared custody more often.

It is noteworthy to mention that contemporary women are often just as likely to work outside the home as men. Therefore, women no longer have the traditional advantages over men of having more time available to dedicate to child rearing, and can no longer support the argument that they have more experience as a child's caretaker. As a result, less weight is given to those aspects when formulating a custody order.

Courts are also more likely to grant shared custody when the parties can effectively communicate with each other and are congenial. Further, parties who live relatively close to one another, which reduces the child's travel time between the parties and may enable the selection of a school district to be undisputed, are more likely to receive shared custody.

Common Challenges in Child Custody Cases

The most complicated custody cases tend to be those where the parents are the most emotionally charged. One might presume the complicated cases are those involving abuse, drug use, or other type of dangerous behavior. Those cases are complicated in many ways because of the nature of the situation, but despite their apparently complex nature they can be somewhat simple because the "good guy" and "bad guy" are clear, especially if the parent with the problems is not taking any steps to resolve them. The obvious approach to these cases involves gathering the facts to prove the "good guy" is the parent fighting for the children, and the "bad guy" is the one committing the abusive or dangerous behavior, and the solution is removing the child from that situation and suggesting counseling.

Cases where the parents are similarly situated, yet elect to engage in a highly litigious custody case, tend to be deceptively complex because they involve subtle nuances and refined factual issues to distinguish the parties. Practitioners must examine these cases carefully to try to find a way to distinguish the client from the opposing parent, and then once the differences are found, argue them in a way that would convince the judge that they are weighty and convincing.

Providing legal counsel to clients in these cases is also tricky. Clients in such matters tend to be extremely emotionally invested and view what are, to the objective observer, subtle differences between the parents as deep gulfs and wide chasms, and they expect their attorneys to be sympathetic to their causes and share their same view of the issues. Practitioners must interact with their clients with skill, subtlety, and wisdom. It takes grace and skill to communicate to clients who view the adversary as the "bad guy" that the matters at issue do not have the significance the clients apply to them and that the opposing party is not so "bad." Dealing with this type of client requires experience with interacting with people in this sort of emotional state, understanding them, and anticipating how they will respond to advice. As in divorce cases, clients often experience a variety of emotions during the legal process, and they want their lawyers to be sympathetic and be willing to go along for what is often a turbulent ride. It is part of a lawyer's role to stand up to clients who are unreasonable, either in their expectations of what the court system can or will do for them, or in the amount and type of input the clients want to exert in a case. It is important to remember though that sometimes standing up to clients will cause them to examine their behavior and thought processes. This can be helpful as clients can become so emotionally involved in their cases that they fail to think rationally about problems. Lawyers should not be "talking heads." If you do not agree with a client, it is sometimes good to suggest parting ways if there are too many divergent views that cannot be resolved.

Mistakes Parents Make in Custody Battles

It is not surprising that the biggest mistakes parents make during custody battles are: (1) feeling that they are the "best" parent, and the other parent should not have any, or very limited custody rights; (2) viewing the custody litigation as a "battle;" (3) losing perspective; and, (4) failing to understand how to apply past parenting behaviors to future parenting behaviors.

Attorneys frequently receive calls from clients (usually mothers) who insist that they are the "best" parent because of things they did for the child(ren) and things that the other parent allegedly did or did not do. They want to proceed to court to eliminate the rights of the other parent based on these thoughts. Attorneys should educate these potential or current clients that this is a poor attitude, and that a judge will often react to that attitude by limiting their own custodial rights. Attorneys should consider refusing to represent clients if the "my way or the highway" attitude continues. Also, although these parents insist that their child(ren) shares their attitude and wants nothing to do with the alleged offending parent, these parents have often been surprised to hear their child(ren) testify in court to the opposite, and in fact, voice a preference to live with the allegedly offending parent. Studies have indicated that no matter how much of a perceived "bum" a parent is, a child still feels a strong pull to have a relationship with both parents. It is important to always remember that the dispute between the parents usually will not cause a child to stop loving either one.

Although many people approach custody litigation as a "battle," doing so is an enormous mistake in terms of bringing the matter to a sensible resolution and ensuring the well-being of the children at issue. Obviously, if there is litigation over custody, there is some dispute between the parties regarding how custody of the children should be divided between them. Despite the presence of the dispute, however, the litigation does not necessarily have to deteriorate into a battle. The parties can certainly present legitimate arguments and issues over which there is an impasse that only a judge can decide, but it is a mistake to turn a legitimate legal dispute into a battle. The difference between a legitimate legal dispute and a battle is that, in a battle, the parties focus on issues of minutiae, spite, and revenge. Battles tend to involve being angry, making illogical decisions, stonewalling over minor issues, constantly rehashing the past as opposed to looking toward the future, and pursuing ends for their own gain as opposed to pursuing the best interests of the children. The best approach is to tone down the emotion and ill feelings toward the opposition and focus solely on the children. Attorneys have the opportunity to counsel their clients to think more rationally and redirect their efforts and feelings to more productive and appropriate goals. Suggesting counseling with a licensed therapist is always a good idea when logic and reason fall short.

Clients involved in custody litigation are generally emotionally invested in the case, but they sometimes lose perspective altogether. This emotional charge naturally tends to distort a client's view of the case and its issues. The symptoms of losing perspective include overemphasizing issues of lesser significance, failing to let go of incidents from the past (and sometimes the distant past), and assuming the unpleasant interactions between the parents predict how a parent will interact with the children.

Finally, many clients fail to properly apply past parenting to future parenting. This happens in two ways: (1) the client turns what was apparently acceptable behavior in the past into allegedly salient current issues, and (2) presuming a lack of experience doing certain things means a near impossibility of doing them in the future. An example is when both parents and the child live with the child's grandparents for a period of years and during the entire time one of the grandparents smokes marijuana. The parents eventually split up, with one parent remaining with the child in the grandparents' home. The parent living elsewhere goes to an attorney with the outwardly serious complaint that the child has to live in an environment in which smoking marijuana is condoned. The irony that the client misses is that the now complaining parent apparently had no problem living in that environment for a significant period of time, but now that the parents are divided, it is an issue. The complaining client's mistake is failing to understand decisions from the past are compromising their current position. An attorney should try to correct this illogical thinking as much as possible.

When parents are together, they will naturally divide the labor of raising their children. For example, when a child is young, often the mother takes the lead with feeding, diapers, middle-of-the-night care, and naps. Just because the mother took the lead in these areas when the parents were together does not mean that it is logical, assumed, or obvious that the father is incapable of assuming these responsibilities now that they are separated. Again, the attorney should try to disabuse a client of this sort of faulty logic.

Challenges for Plaintiffs in Child Custody Cases

The challenges faced by custody plaintiffs in settling cases are not much different from those in other sorts of cases. A custody plaintiff, like the plaintiff in most other types of case, bears the burden of proof and the odds of that plaintiff proving a case certainly can motivate (or disincline) the defendant to settle.

The unique features of a custody case are that the case involves the well-being of another person, and that emotions nearly always run high. A custody plaintiff must demonstrate that the terms of settlement are not for the benefit of the plaintiff or to spite the opposing party, but is in the best interests of the child(ren). A custody plaintiff must also ensure that the ends sought are legitimate and not borne out of an overly emotional approach to the case.

The attorney must carefully evaluate the facts of the case, but just as importantly, the attorney must also keep an objective perspective about the case to ensure that while emotions may run high, logic and rational thinking prevail. Attorneys face a challenge in providing objective advice gently and with compassion to the clients, telling them things they may not want to hear. It is a difficult balance to strike, as clients may get the impression that the attorney is advocating against them for the other parent. It is important for the attorney to ensure that while providing the objective advice, the attorney is not arguing against the client, but is preparing them for the arguments they may have to face.

Successful Custody Case Outcomes

The best outcome of a custody case involves putting the children in the best situation possible following the case, allowing the parents to be as effective as possible in rearing the child, and working with one another to that end. How an order or settlement plays out to that end is different in each case, as every set of parents presents a new and different set of variables. Regardless of these differences, there is always an arrangement that best serves the child(ren) in the case and that arrangement, regardless of whether the client "won," is success in a custody case.

Recent Notable Custody Cases

Five cases decided in the past year have had a notable effect in the context of custody cases.

Case 1: C.M.K. v. K.E.M.[1] Pennsylvania's new custody statute took effect in January 2011. The statue established new standards for custody relocation. The Pennsylvania Superior Court established two important precedents in this case. First, a party that takes the initiative in requesting a relocation in a case that may not be a relocation does not, by so requesting, implicitly

[1] *C.M.K. v. K.E.M.*, 45 A.3d 417 (Pa. Super. Ct. 2012).

concede that the matter is a relocation case. In other words, a court will not automatically presume a case is a relocation matter simply because someone requests a relocation. Second, the Court made it clear that a case, even if it involves literally relocating a child, would not be considered a relocation case if the move does not "significantly impair" the non-relocating parent. Furthermore, when determining whether a move would significantly impair custody, the court looks at more than just the number of hours spent by a parent with the child but also the "quality" of the custody as well.

Case 2: K.E.M. v. P.C.S.[2] was heard by the Pennsylvania Supreme Court. The standard rule in Pennsylvania is that a child born to a marriage is presumed to be the offspring of the same. The *K.E.M.* Court ruled that the aforesaid presumption ought not serve as an absolute bar to pursue a biological father for support when the presumptive father exists. Instead, the Court ruled that the aforesaid presumption is rebuttable if it would serve the best interests of the child at issue.

Case 3: In re S.J.[3] was heard by the Pennsylvania Superior Court. This case dealt with whether the custody order issued in the context of a dependency action is actually permanent, despite an order describing itself as such. Although the court issued an order of permanent physical custody, the Pennsylvania Superior Court also admitted that this order could be changed or modified in the future if the biological mother of the child at issue attempted to file for custody at some point in the future when she resolved the issues impeding her ability to have custody at the time of the ruling.

Case 4: J.R.M. v. J.E.A.[4] This case, which was heard in Pennsylvania Superior Court, is another case that was among the first to apply and interpret the new Pennsylvania custody statute that took effect in January 2011. The new custody statute requires the judge issuing a custody order to do so with a detailed order or explanation of the same from the bench. The Superior Court ruled that the order issued by the Common Pleas Court was too cryptic and did not account for the factors to determine custody as laid out by the new custody statute. The Superior Court noted that the lower court did not make any clear or detailed findings of fact

---

[2] *K.E.M. v. P.C.S.*, 38 A.3d 798 (2012).
[3] *In re S.J.*, 64 A. 3d 32 (Pa. Super. Ct. 2012).
[4] *J.R.M. v. J.E.A.*, 33 A.3d 647 (Pa. Super. Ct. 2011).

that would enable it to determine what factors were used to support the custody order. Therefore, the Superior Court remanded the matter for the lower court to conduct more findings of fact and prepare a detailed order explaining its ruling.

Case 5: The Pennsylvania Superior Court case of *E.D. v. M.P.* is the first reported case interpreting the relocation section of Pennsylvania's new custody statute, which took effect in January 2011.[5] One of the parties in this matter attempted relocation without following the procedures under the new statute. Evidently, the pursuit of the custody modification in this matter started its life before the new statute went into effect. The Superior Court ruled that the relocation requirements under the statue would not apply to matters initiated before it went into effect. Furthermore, as with *J.R.M. v. J.E.A*, the Court remanded the matter so the trial court could issue an order with the specificity required by the new statute.[6]

Common Paternity Issues

Paternity issues are rather straightforward. They all begin with one of the parties, if not both, questioning the parentage of a child or children. The suspicious party has the option of filing a petition requesting a paternity test. Most petitions are uncontested, so the non-petitioning parent agrees to allow the test to go forward. Of those that are contested, the party seeking the test must present a rational basis for the suspicion and request for the test. Test petitions are generally granted, especially to unwed parents.

Children can benefit from their knowing their paternity because there is an inherent virtue and value to knowing one's parents. Further, men who specifically seek to discern paternity with the hope that the test returns a positive result are often very involved and interested parents who work hard at being fathers.

Complications usually revolve around unexpected test results. Following unexpected results, it is important to counsel clients and help them work through the fact that a party is or is not the father. Further, if a man who had previously not been believed to be a child's father is proven to be one

[5] *E.D. v. M.P.*, 33 A.3d 73 (Pa. Super. Ct. 2011).
[6] *See*, *J.R.M. supra* n. 4.

through a paternity test, the mother must accept the fact that he will likely want some type of custody for the first time, even if the child is older. It may also be prudent to suggest counseling for children, especially older ones, who suddenly learn that their perceived fathers are not actually their biological fathers or vice versa.

There was a situation we dealt with in which a child—now in her late twenties—had been raised by her mother and another man she thought was her father, who was married to her mother. The child was told by her mother that another man may be her biological father, because she was experiencing similar health problems as those experienced by that man. Although we cautioned the possible biological father that his willingness to take a paternity test could result in the child making a claim to be part of his substantial estate, he took the test. It was determined that he was the likely biological father, and he has embraced a relationship with his new daughter. He decided to provide for her in his estate, but his daughters from his marriage are upset about the relationship as this new person, heretofore a non-family member, is now suddenly encroaching on their share of the estate.

Role of the Client in Family Law Cases

Obviously, the client plays the central role in the pursuit of a custody matter. After meeting with a client and asking general questions about the matter, we always ask the client to write a detailed narrative of all the events and important issues in chronological order. This enables clients to collect their thoughts and gives us a relatively reliable account of all of the relevant events and issues. We also find that a narrative of this sort gives us a measure of security in case the client takes issue with our representation. We can always refer to the narrative and its contents if the client complains that other details should have been included at a hearing or court filing.

Clients often approach cases with no self-awareness of their own life issues that may present problems in securing custody. No one is perfect, and there is an argument against virtually everyone having custody. Effective representation in a custody case is offensive, in that one attempts to describe the other parent as inadequate, but also defensive, in that one attempts to describe one's own client as a good parent and explain away the arguments against that client. While most arguments may not be negative, it is important to encourage the client to anticipate the negative things the other parent could say about him/her in court. This is a good exercise both to encourage self-awareness and preparation for arguments against the client.

Clients also frequently forget that the case is not about the parents, and instead is about the children at issue. It is not unusual for a client to relate all manner of negative things about the other parent, but, very often, these negative things reflect on the relationship between the parents as opposed to actual parenting issues. We often remind our clients that while it is clear that they dislike one another and, indeed, may treat one another poorly, this dislike or poor treatment does not necessarily translate to problematic or questionable parenting.

Succeeding in Family Law

A good family law attorney must be a good counselor, listener, and, in many cases, a good therapist; in addition, he/she must be compassionate and empathize with clients. Good attorneys in this area of law have the ability to understand when clients' emotional investments are irrational. It is important not just to have these qualities, but to demonstrate them to the clients and make them believe that the attorney has a good grasp on the clients' feelings in addition to the facts.

Unlike other areas of the law, a custody case is about winning for a third party, the children at issue, as opposed to one's client. The case is about proving what is in the best interests of the children, not just achieving what the client most wants. One hopes that the client's desired ends are what are best for the children, but sometimes they are not. It takes a good family attorney to help a client see and understand that.

A successful family attorney must also be intuitive and wise enough to "read between the lines" of what the parents are presenting. In many—if not most—custody cases, the parents will relate stories of situations that are diametrically opposed. Sometimes it is hard to believe that they are relating the same incident or issue. A successful family attorney must see past these stories for an accurate picture of what happened.

A successful family attorney must also have good trial skills, as custody cases will often go to trial. Knowing how best to present objections, arguments, and testimony will go a long way to win cases. Finally, a successful family attorney is one who can think "outside the box." There are many ways to resolve a custody case and many ways a custody order can be structured. Similarly, there are many ways to divide up marital property and use alimony not just as a means of support, but as a way to practically equalize property division when splitting the available assets. It is vitally important for the family attorney to keep all options on the table without any imposed limitations of previous cases, court "custom," or a client's expectations. Often the best solution is the innovative one that provides a global settlement of issues.

Advice for Attorneys Working Through Child Custody Disputes

As mentioned earlier, we encourage our clients to draft a narrative of their experiences with the children at issue and the other parent, and all other relevant issues. We also help them to take an honest assessment of themselves and their own parenting so that we can attempt to anticipate the arguments from the other parent. Once this data is collected, we attempt to walk our clients through what they can reasonably expect from a custody order. We also attempt to prepare them for the allegations that will be made against them in a custody order. We think such preparation is important for two reasons. First, it is healthy for clients to have as satisfactory and accurate a view of themselves as possible. Specifically, this enables clients to have reasonable expectations of not just the case but also of their own ability to parent without the other parent's direct involvement. Second, it also helps the client anticipate hearing these unpleasant allegations made in open court and to prepare a reasonable, calm, and measured reaction to them. The last thing one wants is for one's client to have an outburst in court. It is never helpful in any way, and is often a hindrance.

While religion and nationality differences only occasionally play a significant role in custody cases, sometimes parents of different cultural backgrounds have different expectations of parental roles. If both parents agree on those roles, the case can proceed relatively smoothly. If not, the dispute or conformity with American cultural standards can make for a difficult transition. Similarly, the roles of the genders, although evolving, are still viewed traditionally. Women, as the typical primary caretakers and parents with fewer working hours (and, therefore, more time available for the child) tend to be primary custodians of children, especially when they are younger. However, men are becoming more active and participatory with their children which, in the long run, will be beneficial for their children, while women are becoming more career-oriented. Therefore, the old-fashioned presumptions of gender roles are increasingly obsolete.

Clients who are emotionally upset need their space. They need to know that their emotions are understandable and normal. Custody cases are traumatic. They bring up all manner of embarrassing and negative things about someone, only to have them aired in public in front of strangers and possibly friends, family, co-workers, and employees. Custody cases bring out the innate aggressive response parents have when they perceive their children are in danger. Such a response may not always be rational or productive and it is important to help the client redirect this response to something more appropriate, such as finding ways to help the children get through the case and working toward a solution with the other parent. Finally, it is almost always difficult for a parent who may have spent time with the children virtually every day to be told by a stranger (i.e., the judge) that future contact will be limited in some way. It is important to explain to the client the realities of sharing custody between two people in different households. It presents challenges for all parties involved, especially the child(ren), and it is the parents' responsibility to make the situation as smooth and uneventful as possible for the child(ren) involved.

On occasion, in the more severe cases, we will suggest the client seek therapy. Sometimes the wounds of the parental relationship are so deep, and affect the custody case so profoundly, that we cannot deal with them as an attorney. Dealing with wounds like these requires a mental health professional's assistance. It is important for this treatment to occur because the issues distort the client's perception and the client acts out of sheer emotion instead of reason.

Establishing Amounts of Child Support

For most cases, the amount of child support is established by a set of guidelines the state legislature developed for use across the Commonwealth of Pennsylvania. The guidelines begin with a combined adjusted net monthly income for both parents of $900, and go all the way up to an adjusted net monthly income of $30,000. Obviously, with such an enormous expanse between the low figure and the high figure, practically everyone who applies for support will be within the guidelines.

For a case that falls within the guidelines, there is no analysis of whether the support amount will adequately cover a child's needs. The guidelines firmly establish the Commonwealth's, and therefore the law's, position that whatever support amount the guidelines dictate is considered sufficient to adequately cover a child's needs.

In very few limited cases a "deviation" from the guidelines will be permitted. Such deviations are for reasons such as an unusual amount of other income in the household (e.g., a new spouse or co-habitant), other support obligations, or other needs and fixed obligations. It should be noted that a deviation is only permitted if these other factors are unusual or out of someone's control. Therefore, the fact that an obligor cannot pay for his $700-a-month car payment because he elected to drive a Porsche, or cannot pay his extremely high mortgage because he elected to live in a very expensive neighborhood, will not justify the deviation from the guidelines.

In the cases of earnings below $900 a month, the courts view them on a case-by-case basis and look at the relative incomes of the parties. If the obligor simply cannot pay due to poverty, then an order of something extremely nominal or even nothing will be entered. In the cases above $30,000 a month, the courts have an alternative set of calculations to determine a support figure.

Child support is always appropriate, as children always have needs and justice and fairness dictates that those needs ought to be supported by both parents. The only cases where child support may not be offered are in cases where the parties share custody equally and their incomes are sufficiently similar so as to make a support order inherently inequitable and unfair to the obligor.

Building a Custody Case

Building a custody case involves three main components: (1) discerning what is best for the child; (2) pursuing the arguments that present your client in the best light possible; and (3) pursuing arguments that present the other parent in a poor light.

Achieving the best interests of the child is paramount, as that is the goal of the court and the custody process in general. The precise details of what are the best interests of a child differ with each case as each child is unique and has unique needs. Generally, however, best interests of a child are fairly intuitive: a loving and stable environment, proper hygiene and nutrition, sufficient housing, sufficient resources, a good education, and healthy family relationships. The issue in a custody case is what sort of custodial split between the parents best achieves the above for the child.

Once the best interests of the child are discerned, the attorney must attempt to pursue the arguments that best suggest one's own client can meet these needs better than the other parent. A custody case is not any different than any other sort of court case in that if a party makes an assertion, it is important to find, develop, and present any and all evidence that supports that assertion. Evidence can include testimony, school records, health records, police records, psychiatric or counseling records, and photographs. For example, an attorney can demonstrate to the court that one's own client can provide a more loving and stable environment than the other parent through presenting evidence of time spent with the child by a parent or by presenting evidence that the other parent is neglectful, abusive, or perhaps simply not quite as involved. Through testimony, the attorney can reveal to the court that the child eats and bathes properly. Photographs of the home or even a formal home study go a long way toward proving what sort of housing and resources are available to a child when in a particular parent's custody. Of course, school records or studies comparing the quality of the parent's preferred schools will help a court determine which parent can best further the child's schooling. Witnesses can also testify about how the parents treat the child, what the child does, and how the child behaves and interacts with others. This can be powerful evidence of what is or is not in a child's best interests.

Finally, it is important to keep in mind that the children can be the most potent weapon in favor of or against one's client's case. The children are eyewitnesses to virtually everything regarding their own custody. They can testify to a judge about everything that happens with the parents, how they feel about it, and what they want. The risk lies in accurately predicting what the children will say when given the opportunity to testify. Many clients insist on calling a child as a witness, convinced that they know exactly how the child will testify, only to be gravely disappointed when the child testifies exactly the opposite of what they predicted, or testifies with much less anger, zeal, intensity, or significance than anticipated on a given issue. Asking a child to testify is not just risky, but also potentially damaging to the child, as the child will have to testify, in theory at least, "against" his parents, knowing that both of his parents have some expectation of support. Being negative in public about one's own parents is traumatic enough, let alone knowing that the testimony may also disappoint the parent or, from a child's point of view, "get them in trouble" in some way. The decision to make a child testify must be made carefully. While it could ultimately secure what is best for the child, it could also harm both the case and the child. Always remember that children love their parents and, in all likelihood, will continue to do so, regardless of the circumstances and result of the custody case.

Conclusion

Each custody case must be approached on a case-by-case basis, with great care taken to ensure what is best for the child(ren), as opposed to the parents, is the priority. Custody cases are extremely emotionally charged, so it is imperative to help one's clients to be able to appropriately and adequately deal with and direct their emotions in the most productive and helpful way. Keeping a client's expectations and perspective on his custody case will go a long way to keeping the custody litigation moving smoothly, rationally, and hopefully will result in a benefit for the child(ren) at issue.

Key Takeaways

- Joint custody arrangements have become a more common element of custody orders. The role of each parent in a child's life is more respected, especially the role of the father.
- Custody cases where the parents are similarly situated tend to be deceptively complex because the attorney must find a way to distinguish the client from the opposing parent.

- Among mistakes parents make during custody battles are feeling that they are the "best" parent and trying to severely limit the other parent's rights, viewing the custody litigation as a "battle," and losing perspective.
- Unlike other areas of the law, a custody case is about winning it for a third party, the children at issue.

Faye Riva Cohen, owner of the Law Office of Faye Riva Cohen PC, is licensed to practice in Pennsylvania who has been practicing law since 1974. She is the president and managing attorney of both the Law Office of Faye Riva Cohen PC and Legal Research, Inc.

Acknowledgment: *James W. Cushing is an associate at the Law Office of Faye Riva Cohen PC licensed to practice in Pennsylvania who has been practicing law since 2002. He is a research attorney for Legal Research, Inc.*

The Intricacies of the Attorney-Client Relationship and Their Roles During Representation

Tracey L. Rosswurm

Owner

The Law Office of Tracey L. Rosswurm LLC

ASPATORE

Introduction

The symbiotic relationship of the attorney and client is comprised of necessary components such as competency, communication, case management, and candor. A successful, professional relationship will consist of equal contributions so that the goals of representation can be attained.

In my family law practice, which consists of providing legal services for enforcement, dissolution of marriage, modifications of custody, support and parenting time, adoptions, and protective orders, whether I am working as an arbitrator, mediator or representing a client, I have seen time and time again that people just want to be heard. They want to tell their side of the story. They want someone to listen and they want finality.

The ever-changing world of technology, social media, and an unpredictable economy continue to present new and interesting challenges for the attorney-client relationship. Information is so easily accessible via the Internet, and thus, the attorney and the client each generally have an expectation of promptness. Moreover, clients have a desire to plot the course of their case because they have funded the matter. Although it is the attorney's job to navigate by determining strategy, the attorney must do so in a way to capture and retain the client's trust. After all, the client can choose any attorney. Regardless, the attorney-client relationship is a complicated one and likely to continue to become more complex. Understanding the mutual role that the client and the attorney each play is a fundamental part of any case.

The Role of the Client in a Family Law Case

The primary role of the client in a family law case is three-fold: (1) to provide an abundance of information to the attorney to support and advance their legal pursuit; (2) to do it in a timely manner; and (3) to be cognizant of the costs—emotional and financial—that the action will take on the client, the client's family, and their children.

Though the attorney will never have a complete picture of the family's dynamics and history, the client will need to provide sufficient information to create an elaborate picture for the attorney. This will allow the attorney to present the most effective and successful case possible to the mediator, and/or opposing counsel and/or to the judge. The decision makers can only render a fair and accurate decision based upon the information presented, and in large part, this is possessed by the client.

Rendering a favorable decision cannot occur if the client's goal is to give distortions of the truth about their case or by failing to impart seemingly inauspicious information about him/herself. For example, if a client explains a custody situation in which the client does no wrong and all fault is on the other parent, this will not be helpful to the attorney.

The client's ability to provide information about himself/herself and the circumstances that are uncomfortable to talk about or that are unbecoming is crucial. It also bestows credibility to the client. It is not uncommon that clients do not want to disclose information about their life or behavior that would cause one to question their morality, whether it is infidelity, addiction, or a criminal background, for example. A client's disclosure of being infected by a sexually transmitted disease is embarrassing and incredibly personal. It would be easier for a client to keep that information to his or herself. But by disclosing such information in a proactive rather than a reactive manner, there could be legal remedies that are available for that client. It is the attorney's job to solicit information from the client. The best way to do this is to assure the client that you are not here to pass judgment on them, their life, or their behavior. The more information that the attorney has from the onset of the case, the better position the client is in. There is nothing worse than learning negative things about your client from the adversary on the day of a hearing.

Oftentimes the information requested of the client can be tedious to obtain, time-consuming, and just plan inconvenient. Understanding the reasons behind the information request is helpful and can provide motivation for the client in expediting procurement of information. The best place for a client to start is to provide a narrative account of the circumstances that led up to the legal action. The client's sacrifice of time in obtaining information and detail given by the client for the attorney displays a level of commitment to the legal process.

The most informative narrative will consist of a detailed and elaborate depiction of the events that occurred that gave rise to the legal action, including dates, times, and geographic locale of the occurrence. Also, names and addresses of witnesses and efforts taken by the client to mitigate damages are equally important. A chronological timeline of events and the client's supposition of what the adversary would say about the client will round out the narrative.

A good narrative will not consist of adjectives or allegations. For example, "My husband is an irresponsible drunk" is not helpful, versus, "My husband forgets to pick up the children from school because he drinks a case of beer in the afternoon." Clearly, you can see the significance of the distinction.

In addition, recruiting the help of family members and friends is often a resource that can aid the client in gathering necessary information. It also helps the client to have perhaps a different perspective of the issues as well.

Providing the information requested prevents the attorney from having to subpoena information that is easily accessible to the client and it saves the client money that could be used on the client's family and in the client's household.

The client's timeliness in providing information to the attorney is as important as the information itself. The cliché "better late than never" usually is not accurate or helpful in a legal setting. For example, if your client has information that could win your case, it is not helpful if you receive the information after the hearing. However, "time is money" is often accurate. If the client provides the attorney information in a timely manner, it could prevent the attorney from unnecessary work resulting in unnecessary attorney fees. Further, it could accelerate the negotiation process resulting in a more expeditious disposition. A client is not in a position to negotiate when all of the information is not readily available for the attorney. The attorney needs as much information as possible to render good legal advice, thus placing the client in the best position possible.

The attorney is required, at a minimum, to exercise due diligence in verifying information, and ensuring the accuracy of pleadings and representations made to the court. The judicious remittance of information by a client will afford the attorney ample time to comply with such requirements.

The attorney's establishment of a clear timeline for when the client is to provide information is crucial. Even more important is the attorney's duty to follow up on the information requests given to the client. Often a client forgets, does not understand the information request but is too embarrassed to admit it, or needs help in obtaining the information. The attorney should tickle their calendar for compliance. A rigid case management system and a paralegal can assist in removing the element of unpreparedness so on the day of trial there is no stone unturned.

The client must also timely comply with the court's orders. Whether it is paying child support on a certain day of the week, remitting medical expenses to the adversary, or notifying the attorney of an error in an order, the client must be mindful of legal deadlines to avoid losing their rights or being sanctioned.

The costs of a legal action are not just financial. Legal matters take an emotional toll on people as well, regardless of whether the client is initiating or defending the legal action.

The most important questions a client should ask him or herself are, "Can my family and I endure the emotional toll the legal action will pose?" and "Can we afford it financially?"

Many people have work, children, and family to contend with. Legal actions are exceptionally stressful because they are another thing that people have to manage in their daily lives. For many people, the burden is too much to handle and people make the mistake of ignoring legal documents in hopes of it just going away.

Depression, sadness, fear, anxiousness, lack of sleep, and loss of appetite are common problems often reported that are associated with a legal action. If feeling overwhelmed, the client should seek the intervention of a professional, such as a counselor, to help cope so he or she can continue to manage daily affairs.

Having emotional support to deal with the emotional issues associated with a legal action is important for a client so that the client's thinking is lucid as to legal decisions and so the client has the ability to keep his or her family intact. Legal problems, without the help of resources, such as an attorney or a counselor, can interfere with a client's ability to adequately perform at work, thus potentially resulting in employment termination/loss of income and perhaps an inability to proceed with the legal action.

A client that says, "I don't care what it costs, I want to bury them in court," is thinking in a way not grounded in logic. Such an attitude can be emotionally and financially exhausting for a client and for the attorney. An attorney should avoid representing the type of client who is out for revenge or retaliation. This type of client is often never satisfied and may turn against you in their retaliation endeavors.

The Initial Client Meeting

The client's experience in coming to the attorney's office should be as pleasant as possible. It is a nerve-racking and scary event for a client or potential client. Whether it is pleasant music, a television, popular magazines, or a cold beverage, these should await each client. These things will help calm the client while he or she completes the initial consultation form (consisting of inquiries regarding the client's general identifying information and the legal issues at hand) and briefly waits for the attorney.

Prior to the attorney meeting with the client, a conflict check should be conducted. The initial meeting should commence with an exchange of pleasantries and a bit of affable conversation. This will allow for a preliminary reciprocal assessment between the client and attorney and it will help the client be put at ease. It is equally important that the attorney determine whether the potential client is someone that the attorney wants to work with.

It is imperative that the attorney listen to the client's concerns and allow the client to talk for a duration that is acceptable to the client. This not only helps the client to feel important, it helps the attorney understand the circumstances from the client's perspective, in addition to the legal perspective. The simplest thing, such as a nod by the attorney or a smile, can indicate compassion and understanding.

Once the client is finished telling their story, the attorney should confirm, succinctly, what she heard the client say and identify the client's concerns and legal issues.

The attorney should provide the client with (a) a detailed and elaborate explanation of the law; (b) how the law applies to the client's circumstance; (c) the strengths of the client's case; (d) the weaknesses of client's case; (e) the relief the client may be entitled to; (f) a timeline of the legal process and procedures involved; (g) strategy in attaining the client's wishes; and (h) the anticipated general costs for pursuing or defending the client's action.

Using legal jargon is not usually educational or helpful to the client. Educating a client about the law is most helpful when it is done in the simplest of terms. If you go to the doctor and the doctor says, "You have pneumonoultramicroscopicsilicovolcanoconiosisi," you will be scratching your head in confusion. However, if your doctor says, "You have lung disease," you can understand that. It is no different in the legal world. As an example, we once had a client whose hearing was continued. Most attorneys understand that a continuance means that the hearing is rescheduled or taken off the court's calendar; however, our client showed up on the day of the hearing, dressed and ready for court. We asked her if she received our notice that her hearing was continued. She responded, "I sure did." We asked why she still appeared knowing that. Her response was, "You said the hearing was continued, so that means we are moving forward with the case, right?" Certainly a fair assumption by her. Had we told her that her hearing was rescheduled rather than saying it was continued, we could have saved her a trip to our office.

An unpleasant thing for most people is giving bad news. Unfortunately, being the bearer of bad news is sometimes a necessary evil for an attorney. Though perhaps not easy, being straightforward is the least painful way of dealing with such a situation. Procrastination in giving the bad news will not likely change the situation. Further, knowledge is power for your client. The sooner your client knows the strengths and weaknesses of his or her case, the sooner that decisions can be made—financial and otherwise. It also helps the client to have realistic expectations about the case and the knowledge necessary to negotiate or determine whether to proceed to trial. Mostly, people just appreciate knowing.

Attorneys are often afraid of committing to an assessment of whether the client's case is weak or strong. If the attorney presents information that indicates the client's case is weak, the attorney faces the possibility of losing the client because the client may go searching for a more favorable assessment elsewhere. If the attorney commits to an opinion that the client has a strong case, often attorneys fear backlash may result from the client if the case does not result in the success anticipated. Detailing the reasons why you believe the client's case is strong or weak will help the client to understand more about the process and the law.

The attorney should also direct the client's attention to various resources available that are particular to that client's needs, such as various local agencies, state agencies, government websites, and to the attorney's website.

If the potential client chooses to hire the attorney, a formal questionnaire is completed and a fee agreement is signed by the client and attorney. The formal questionnaire provides the attorney with preliminary/basic information for opening the client's file, preparing initial pleadings, and initiating various methods of discovery. Discovery is the information-gathering devices that are generally used prior to negotiation or trial. The most common methods are interrogatories, which are questions that are propounded by one party and served upon another party and are to be answered under oath and generally within thirty days from the date of service. Interrogatories are commonly used but are not as flexible as depositions. A deposition is done under oath with a court reporter transcribing the questions and answers and it allows for cross-examination, unlike interrogatories. It is an inexpensive means of establishing important facts. A deposition can be taken of anyone relative to the case whereas interrogatories can only be served upon the parties to an action.

A Request for Production of Documents and Information can be served upon any third party that has information relative to the pending cause of action. It can be served upon the third party fifteen days after the other party has been provided with a copy of the Request to be served. This allows the opportunity for the other party to object. For example, in a child support case, the noncustodial, payor parent's employer may be served with a Request for Production of Documents requesting a copy of that parent's most recent paystub and insurance coverage information. Another example, a child's transcripts or school records could illustrate a trend in the child's emotional downfall or perhaps demonstrate that a parent should not have midweek parenting time because of the tendency of poor grades when in the other parent's care. Whether it is bank statements, children's transcripts, or tax returns, to name a few other examples, these documents will also help the court render a decision based upon the parties' actual circumstances.

A Request for Admission is another discovery method. This is served to the other party for the admission of the truth of any matter relative to the action or the genuineness of any document. It helps to narrow the facts and circumstances. Non-compliance with discovery can result in sanctions and attorney fees.

The formal questionnaire is usually followed up with various requests for additional information so that the client is not overwhelmed at their first consultation. The requests for additional information are usually made via phone call, correspondence or at a client meeting. Sometimes the court will request (via an order) additional information.

The fee contract will ensure that there is a meeting of the minds as to the financial responsibility associated with the client's legal representation. Then, it is time to begin representation—pleadings and/or motions are filed with the court, discovery is initiated, mediation and/or hearings are scheduled, and the case is nurtured with the goal of an expeditious and remarkable resolution.

Questions, Concerns and Misconceptions

The most common question that clients ask is, "What is this going to cost me?" Money is usually each client's biggest concern. Although the inquiry is reasonable, unfortunately it is not one that is easily answered. There are many variables that affect each case and no two cases are alike.

Some of the factors that affect a client's case are (1) the reasonableness of the other party; (2) the reasonableness of the other party's attorney; (3) the reasonableness of the client.

Many clients also make the mistake of listening to folk-wisdom—which is well intended but not usually accurate advice—from friends, family and co-workers. This sometimes results in damage to the case for the attorney to repair, and sometimes fixing legal problems created by listening to folk-wisdom is not possible.

If the other party or client is unwilling to negotiate in good faith or unwilling to compromise, refuses to communicate, does not comply with the court's orders (thus forcing court intervention), does not timely comply with discovery, or does not appear for appointments, hearings or mediation, delay ensues, resulting in more attorney fees.

On the other hand, a client who is willing to bestow to the adversary whatever is requested, and forego all rights or interests, may sound like it would make things easier, but this type of unreasonableness is just as difficult to deal with. We have our clients sign waivers indicating that it is against our advice to forego their rights and to acknowledge in writing what they were advised by us that they could potentially be entitled to. It is sad to see a spouse who agreed not to pursue the pension of the other spouse from their thirty-two-year marriage out of hopes of a reconciliation and the client ends up in financial turmoil.

The financial landscape of a legal matter coupled with the anticipated costs are usually the client's biggest concerns. The good news is that there are some financial certainties associated with the costs of a legal action: (1) the hourly amount that the attorney will charge is generally a pre-set amount; (2) clients who are willing to communicate rather than litigate incur less fees; (3) clients that successfully mediate incur less fees; and (4) clients who contact their attorney weekly rather than daily incur less fees.

Because family law matters are so unique and labor-intensive, a flat-fee charge is generally not used. Family law matters usually entail billing in 1/10 of an hour to ensure precision; however, the attorney's hourly rate and the initial retainer are things that should be discussed and determined at the very first meeting with the client.

A client willing to communicate will incur less legal fees because this type of client is usually reasonable and able to understand and consider the pros and cons of their case, thus allowing for good decision making and eliminating decisions based purely on emotion. Plus, clients who are involved in the decision-making aspects of their case are usually more satisfied with the outcome because it probably resulted via a settlement agreement or mediation that they were directly involved in negotiating the outcome of, whereas people who litigate and leave the decision to a judge are more likely to have issue with the outcome because of their lack of involvement.

Mediation usually results in less attorney fees than proceeding to trial because the costs associated with trial (including but not limited to research, ongoing motion and pleading filing, meeting with witnesses, preparation of witnesses for examination, preparation of witnesses for cross-examination, ongoing discovery, and the trial itself) can be very costly. If mediation is successful, a lot of the above-referenced fees and costs are eliminated or significantly reduced.

Although communication with your client is important, it should also be done efficiently. For each meeting or phone call with a client, the file must be pulled and information reviewed and analyzed. If this is done daily, it can be costly, whereas done once a week would likely equate to less attorney fees. The reasonable passage of time will also allow issues that may not necessarily require legal advice to resolve themselves. A common problem in the family law arena is a client who calls the attorney because they fear the other parent will not do something they were ordered to do. The anticipated offense has not even occurred yet. In situations like this the attorney will need to do some emotional hand-holding with the client until if and when a legal problem arises.

Undoubtedly, the client is an indispensable party in the legal matter with the responsibility of providing the fuel for the journey. Having a good relationship with the attorney and complying with the attorney's requests and following the attorney's advice make for a much smoother ride to the destination.

Conclusion

The attorney and the client must work together. They must have open and straightforward communication, understanding, and share the same goals. Reciprocal trust will help pave the way to a smooth conclusion and moderate legal costs.

These essential tasks can be easily accomplished by discussing expectations, procedure, the law, and the emotional and financial aspects of the case at the initial meeting, and the utilization of an effective case management system.

Key Takeaways

- The client's main role is to timely provide information to the attorney and to listen to the advice of the attorney.
- The client should be aware of the financial and emotional toll of a legal action.
- Successful case management equates to attorney preparedness.
- Utilization of various methods for reducing legal costs is essential.
- Putting the client at ease makes for a smoother ride to the disposition.

Tracey L. Rosswurm, owner of the Law Office of Tracey L. Rosswurm LLC, has appeared as a guest on WGN radio (twice) to discuss destination divorce and is the subject of several newspaper and magazine articles. Ms. Rosswurm received her associate degree as a paralegal from Vincennes University. She received her BA degree in criminal justice from Indiana University-Purdue University and her juris doctorate from Thomas M. Cooley Law School. Ms. Rosswurm is a member of IACP and the Family Law Section of the Allen County Bar Association. She is a registered mediator and former family law arbitrator.

Dedication: *To all of the attorneys who strive to enhance the honor and tradition of our profession and to the clients who allow us to serve them.*

Working in the Children's Best Interests in Custody Cases

Gloria Mitchell

Owner

Mitchell Law Group

Introduction

As traditional family roles have shifted and changed over time, so have trends in family law. From historical times, where women and children were actually viewed by society as a man's "property," to today, where we see mothers in the workforce and fathers staying home with young children, the court's view on child custody has evolved with these societal changes. As, unfortunately, separation and divorce are widely present in today's society, knowledge of innovative family law techniques is of vital importance to best represent the interests of gendered clients and their children.

Each and every family law case comes with unique clients, facts, and histories. This chapter will discuss the trends in child custody, varying custody arrangements, and alternative dispute resolution options available in settling family law-related disputes that allow each party to keep the children's best interests at the forefront. While there is not a specific formula any one family law case can follow, having a working knowledge of the various trends and alternative dispute resolution options will allow for a greater breadth of possible strategies that can be used to obtain a positive outcome for each individual involved.

Historical Trends in Child Custody

Early twentieth century doctrine included a concept referred to as the "tender years" presumption, which compelled a finding that children under the age of ten should always be placed with their mothers. This was premised on generalized beliefs that younger children would not develop emotionally without the daily direct influence of the mother. This led to automatic placement of children with the mother in custody battles, or more aptly, removed fathers from waging custody battles by discouraging them from seeking court awarded custody in any circumstance. Prior to this trend, children were viewed as chattel, or "property," belonging to the father, and women were similarly considered chattel, who could not own other property—including their own children. This early myth perpetuated throughout nineteenth century English law, on which our American jurisprudence is based. Historically, even when common thought began to evolve, recognizing that a woman was capable of parenting her child, divorced women were left with insufficient or no financial resources with which to support their children.

During the early 1900s, parents often assumed traditional roles. Fathers worked outside the family home, earning more than half, or all, of the family's wages while the mothers stayed home and filled the role of the children's caretaker. As a result, by the 1920s, forty-eight states had accepted the tender years presumption. However, none of these extremes actually valued or considered the general concept known as the "children's best interests." Over time, as society changed and evolved, more mothers reentered the workforce and shared family responsibilities became more common. Today, far more homes are two-income homes, which has led to the tender years presumption being phased out and flatly rejected by the legal community. Our changing society, the increasing number of men demonstrating parenting skills comparable to women's, and the prevalence of women in the workforce have led to judges becoming more inclined to award custody to fathers if the facts support this conclusion.

Despite these changing factors, the belief is still widely held that it is very difficult for fathers to get custody. However, fathers are being awarded custody in the right cases, and more often today, due not only to a grassroots movement to be recognized as capable parents, but also because they are more willing to seek custody and take their cases to attorneys and to the courtroom. This trend has fluctuated over the past fifteen or twenty years and was further influenced by a theory known as "parental alienation syndrome." In the early 1980s, Richard A. Gardner based this thesis on empirical studies showing nearly all parents who alienated their children from the other parent were women. As a result, lawyers and child psychologists routinely accepted custody cases for fathers and demonstrated to the court that mothers were influencing the children to make claims against their fathers, sometimes leading to false allegations of abuse designed to control a custody outcome. As this theory gained ground, the pendulum took a hard swing, which resulted in nearly two decades of cases shifting custody to fathers, often through a post-decree modification, based upon "parental alienation syndrome."

Presently, there is still a great deal of debate in the legal community and in the general population about whether the playing field was over-leveled for a period of time when the family law bar realized that some fathers had in fact been denied equal access to the courts. If such an over-adjustment existed, it is now being corrected; however, litigation firms are still growing around the specific concept of protecting fathers' rights. In fact, during the last decade in Indiana, several firms that focus on fathers' rights have emerged and are growing. Today's parents are far more likely to find themselves on a completely neutral and level field in the courtroom. As a result, parents are far more likely to find themselves in a joint custody arrangement, which requires both parents to put aside presumptions and generalizations, and instead place their focus on the best interests of their children by engaging in shared parenting and shared communications relating to their children.

The Best Interest of the Child Standard

It was not until the 1970s that fathers first actually *asked* for custody, and not until 1981, in *Devine vs. Devine*,[1] that the tender years presumption was held to be gender biased, violating the Fourteenth Amendment and denying fathers equal protection of the law. However, even before the tender years presumption was struck down as unconstitutional, most states had rejected the tender years doctrine and replaced it with the "best interest of the child" standard. In Indiana, as in most states, a child of any age can have an opinion in the custody battle, but the court gives the child's opinion more weight if he or she is fourteen years of age or older. The age of the child is only one of many non-exclusive factors that the court considers in making custody determinations. Other factors include the parents' wishes and the child's environment, including the school, community, and extended family.

In the early 1990s, the American Psychological Association became involved in custody litigation, and custody litigators entered into cooperative relationships with custody evaluators, teaching classes, conducting cooperative seminars, and involving evaluators in the cases as experts. Before that point, the evaluator's role was largely limited to conducting the necessary psychological testing, writing evaluations, and when necessary, testifying in court. In the 1990s, however, evaluators were more frequently brought into cases to act as consultants and render opinions that did not favor either parent, but rather

[1] *Devine v. Devine*, 398 So. 2d 686 (Ala. Ct. App. 1981).

involved recommending a parenting plan for the unique family dynamic at hand. This proved to be extremely valuable, particularly in cases involving children with special needs, as these recommendations began at a time when there were increasing numbers of diagnoses of behavioral issues, most commonly autism, Asperger's syndrome, and attention deficit hyperactivity disorder. At the same time, parenting decisions about the course of treatment and related options, as well as the correlating use of medication to treat the children, created new issues for families in custody cases. Once the courts began involving mental health professionals in making recommendations relating to the frequency of contact needed by children of different ages with each parent, as well as specific issues such as medications, the tender years doctrine was simply of no use anymore. Instead, professionals began recommending that a child have access to both parents, as the absence of a strong paternal presence during the first ten years of a child's life was finally recognized as a potential damage to a child's development.

In due time, courts began to turn to joint and shared custody as the best way to meet the best interests of the child, as it allows both parents to make the decisions in a child's life and provides the child with equal or comparative access to both parents.

A New "Joint Legal Custody Presumption"

Joint custody stems from the rejection of gender-based presumptions, and relies instead on weighing numerous factors affecting the child, including the wishes and the sex of each parent, the age of the child, the community, the home base, and the primacy of the parent. This weighing of factors often results in a finding that the child is best served by being in the shared and joint custody of both parents. Although it has not yet been mandated by every state legislature, several states have enacted this presumption or are heading directly toward adopting same. The actual presumption of joint legal custody will be the next clear trend and dynamic shift in custody cases. Joint legal custody does not compel joint physical custody—it necessitates the parents to share only in decision making for the child—but joint legal custody and joint physical custody often go together. In 1979, California was the first state to actually enact a joint custody statute, and now every state has one, although they do not yet compel the conclusion that this arrangement is in the best interest of the child. Unquestionably though, many legislatures or State Supreme Courts have created parenting time guidelines and custody laws, all of which clearly tend to recognize that the best interest of a child in a divorce case includes access to, and parenting from, both parents.

Some judges still demonstrate outdated assumptions about whether mothers or fathers should have custody of their children. Additionally, certain counties within a state often do not offer a level playing field, but this will vary based upon the population of each particular community. While there is no longer a gender-based presumption, there is still a presumption that a child's attachment and stability is an important factor in the initial divorce and in a post-divorce modification. In younger children, stability is still a priority, as is bonding with both parents. Thus, it is not uncommon for the mother to have been a stay-at-home parent, making her the primary parent of a young child, and also making her the person most likely to gain custody. The reality is that there are still more mothers who are primary parents than fathers, and while this may arguably appear to embrace the rejected tender years presumption, it is actually a conclusion that meets the best interests standard for the child in many cases.

Creating a Joint-Parenting Arrangement

Some judges feel uncomfortable awarding joint custody if the parties do not agree to it. Indiana's *Pierce v. Pierce*[2] is one of a series of cases in which the court felt that a battleground was inadvertently created through an award of joint legal custody. Forcing two people who are not good communicators to engage in routine conversations and attempt to reach agreements relating to their children can have disastrous results. Custody litigators must be able to consider both sides, and if all is relatively equal, must create a shared parenting and a shared custody arrangement that is satisfactory to everyone. Leaving this task to the judge may result in a decision that is simply unworkable in light of the dynamics of that family. When a child is involved in a divorce, the main focus should always be the child's best interests, not the parent's. The custody litigator should always feel free to have the parents consult with a mental health expert in child-related fields, and

---

[2] *Pierce v. Pierce*, 620 N.E.2d 726 (Ind. Ct. App. 1993).

engage the professional in the process. If the psychologist believes one home is marginally better for the child, this continues to compel a finding that joint custody would best serve that child. Even a slight difference—e.g., four days/three days—will still meet the goals of shared custody and shared parenting.

Attorneys should develop parenting arrangements and agreements that are specific to the facts of each case. An arrangement that may be ideal for one family may not work well for another family. It is important to understand the family dynamics and the specific situation in each case to determine what type of parenting arrangement is in the child's best interest. Some of the most important factors that an attorney should consider are: the age and sex of the child, the emotional and educational needs of a child, sibling and other family bonds, cultural dynamics, whether the parents are able to communicate and cooperate regarding the child, the emotional and psychological health of the parents, the quality of relationship between each parent and the child, and of course the health and safety of the child.

Indiana adopted new parenting-time guidelines in March of 2013. While the guidelines retain the previous manner in which the courts treat children in early infancy (birth to nine months), infants (ten to seventeen months), and toddlers (eighteen months to three years), they are no longer gender specific.[3] Instead, the drafters make nurturing, predictability, stability, and lack of disruption for the child the main priorities. The new parenting-time guidelines presume children of tender years—under the age of five—should spend more time in one home, regardless of whether it is with the mother or the father. Psychologists, parents, family attorneys, and child therapists were involved in writing these new guidelines, and during their discussion groups and panels they considered empirical data that young children have a limited ability to recall people when they are not standing directly in front of them. As a result, the new parenting guidelines aim for more frequent parental visits (versus longer visits) for younger children, and recommend short daily contact to fit the child's limited attention span. As the child ages, the recommendations include more blocks of time with each parent.

[3] IN ST PARENTING TIME GUIDELINES § II.

Parenting Arrangements in High-Conflict Situations

One of the complications of custody litigation is that it is relatively common for parents in divorce or post-divorce situations to refuse to get along, despite advice from family members, friends, child psychologists, judges, and lawyers to the contrary. This is a constant struggle for the family law bar, as judges often charge the lawyers with accountability for making the clients get along with one another. Every family law lawyer has an implied duty to consider the children's interests independently of his or her client, which is often a topic of debate, and which is simply different from other areas of law because as family law attorneys, we work closely with families and children. It is very difficult to try to encourage two high-conflict parents (when you are only able to communicate directly with one of them) to communicate with each other. The courts are often frustrated as they will issue orders, but the orders do not generally end with making two individuals get along if they are not willing to do so. Some clients continually escalate and create drama—arguing in front of the children with no regard to the damage they cause—and this can leave the practitioner feeling ineffective.

I teach a seminar called "high-conflict divorce." Over the past decade I changed the focus of my teaching materials from addressing alienation to coping with high-conflict divorce. Parents demonstrate conflict through ongoing litigation, repeat filings, contempts, anger, and the inability to communicate—behaviors that place the children at risk. In adopting the new guidelines, Indiana has finally acknowledged that high-conflict parents exist, and instead of leaving it to the lawyers and the judges to try to fix the problem, it adopted a concept known as parallel parenting.[4]

Parallel parenting is designed to eliminate or reduce the necessity for contact between two people who have high conflict by limiting their communication to emergencies. Often, communication is further limited to written communication, because if people are forced to e-mail messages, they have the opportunity to re-read the messages and take a moment to bring down the level of hostility before responding, as opposed to hastily making an angry telephone call. Under a parallel

[4] *Id.* § IV.

parenting arrangement, the parents do not have joint legal custody, which requires shared decision making between the parents, but instead, each parent has an equal right to custody. This allows each parent to make the decisions for the child while in his or her care. Parallel parenting is a unique and novel concept, and is therefore largely untested. In approving these guidelines, our Indiana Supreme Court did not intend for parallel parenting to excuse bad behavior or to be a permanent solution. Instead, parallel parenting is intended to act as a bridge during an especially difficult or emotional time—often, the initial divorce phase. Generally, feelings of anger and hostility are more present at the time of the divorce than they are a couple of years later when the parents have remarried or are better able to consider the children's issues rather than their own.

Secondary Effects of Joint Custody Arrangements

While joint custody is gaining recognition as the most beneficial solution for children whose parents are divorced, it does take a toll on both parents. If a woman has been the primary caretaker of her children inside the home for more than ten years, it may be a very harsh transition to compel her into a role in which she is expected to continue to provide the same level of care for her children, while working outside of the home to help support them, and herself, financially. There is no doubt that being removed from the role as a stay-at-home mother in a divorce is disconcerting and frightening, but in those cases the father is also experiencing a transition as he must continue to be the primary breadwinner while also taking on a new role as the children's caretaker. A man who has been used to spending his time working to support his family will learn quickly how difficult it is to work all day and spend evenings cooking meals, preparing for school, and attending the children's extracurricular activities. This is not to say that many parents in these situations do not embrace this change in the dynamics, as it is not uncommon for a mother to be happy to return to the workforce and have the father assume more child-rearing duties. Likewise, many fathers appreciate the opportunity to take a more active role in their children's lives and embrace the parenting plan completely.

Factors Easing the Transition into Co-Parenting

It is a substantial adjustment for parents to transition to a joint custody arrangement, but sharing the responsibility and the duties is in the children's best interest. Historically, problems arose with schools and doctors' offices being willing to share information with both parents, but schools today are doing a better job of informing both parents and allowing children to ride on different buses depending on which parent they are staying with at any given time. Schools have also provided online access to school calendars, which eliminates the problem of one parent receiving the calendar at the beginning of the school year and failing to give it to the other parent. Most public schools have dual access, meaning both parents can obtain passwords to fully participate on the school website. Likewise, doctors' offices offer options that allow two contracts to be signed for dental work such as orthodontia and other medical treatment.

Other changes affecting custody litigation include the use of calendars, parenting plans, and the Internet, which have all made it easier to co-parent. Technological advances in communication, such as Face Time, video chat, and Skype, have had a huge impact on custody litigation. Our increasingly mobile society has led to more relocation cases, but some of the associated issues have been eliminated by technology that allows parents in different states, or even on different continents, to still have face-to-face contact with their children every day at a minimal cost.

Factors Complicating the Transition to Co-Parenting

Prescription dependence and relocation decisions are major factors in joint custody arrangements. Mothers who remarry or achieve great success in their careers are often asked to relocate and travel for their jobs. It is important when confronted with these types of issues to remember that every case is fact-specific and every situation is different. While cases involving a history of domestic abuse or neglect, substance abuse, a poor choice in a current partner, or relocation can be an uphill battle, the court is still likely to award joint custody. It is then left to the attorney to explain that joint custody is likely, despite the other parent's transgressions.

In addition, balanced school calendars, in which students attend school year-round without a summer vacation, can be especially burdensome to a divorced couple trying to co-parent when one parent has relocated. It creates significant additional travel costs because the child can no longer use the summer break to visit with the other parent. While a balanced school calendar is advantageous in that the other parent can see the child more frequently during the year, it also necessitates more plane flights and transportation to make the plan viable.

Parents often have significant trouble transitioning from a two-parent situation to a co-parenting situation. One of the initial burdens many parents face, especially those in high-conflict situations, is coming to terms with the changes in their relationship with the other parent. Depending on the situation, it can sometimes be hard for a parent to move past the hurt or anger they have toward the other parent due to the breakdown in their relationship. In these types of situations, attorneys should consider referring their client to counseling or co-parenting classes that focus on learning how to communicate and co-parent with the other parent. This could benefit the co-parent relationship even if only one parent participates in the counseling or classes. It is important to direct the focus away from the past relationship between the parents to focusing on ensuring the child adjusts well to their new life.

Deciding on a Method of Alternative Dispute Resolution

A variety of types of dispute resolution are available in a child custody case. If the parties have the resources, they may agree to have a private judge (often a retired judge or someone with family law bench experience) hear their case. This can help move the case through the system more quickly—a distinct advantage in an area of law in which delays not only make the case more costly, but also add stress for the children involved. The downside is that a private judge can cost $80 to $100 per hour, but in some cases, it might be worth expending the resources given the alternate price of delaying a case.

Arbitration is another available option, whether it is binding or nonbinding. Nonbinding arbitration, in which the parties submit the case to a panel or a single arbitrator, is usually the better choice in a case in which things are relatively equal. Nonbinding arbitration forces someone to make a decision in a non-adversarial process, and is usually beneficial in child custody cases. Conversely, binding arbitration does not work well for child custody cases, and is certainly no better than presenting the case to a judge and letting the judge decide.

Using Mediation to Determine the Child's Best Interests in a Custody Case

Mediation is unquestionably one of the best ways to handle a child custody case. Mediation provides the parents, who know their family and their routines, more control over the case's outcome. Regardless of the time spent in front of a judge in a custody trial, an attorney can never communicate all of the family's unique characteristics, quirks, patterns, habits, enjoyments, pleasures, and dislikes. Without knowing all of those factors, a judge is hard-pressed to make a decision about the children's best interests. The thought of putting those decisions in the hands of a stranger should make parents take pause and consider mediation. Mediation gives both parents a voice, and also allows the attorneys to invite in an expert to make recommendations for the children, in the child's best interest, instead of asking them to simply testify to "which home is better." The child expert can directly participate in mediation, not as a decision maker but as an advisor to help the parents reach a decision. This can be particularly helpful if a child has a disorder on the autism spectrum, as it allows those special needs to be better incorporated into the parenting plan.

Another benefit of mediation is that the mediator can also approach an older child in a non-adversarial and non-judgmental manner to help the child reach a decision. I have experienced cases where each parent was sure the child's wishes were to live with them. Neither attorney wanted to involve the child in a custody evaluation, but the mediator was able to speak to these children and reach a resolution. Notably, the mediator would report the child had no opinion, loved both parents equally, and did not want to be forced into making any decision, so they did not. Ultimately, joint custody works well for these families, and this could easily be accomplished in mediation, thereby reducing the child's involvement in the process to a brief conversation with the mediator as opposed to the time it would have taken to go to a psychologist's office and have the psychologist testify at court as a witness. Mediation allows the parties to be flexible and uniquely react to issues and create a plan in the best interest of the children. Though mediation has many advantages, it is not appropriate for every case. For example, some may argue that mediation is not always the best option when dealing with cases that involve domestic violence issues. In those types of cases mediation may be used as another tool to control or dominate a victim of family violence. Further, mediation is not always successful and therefore parties will have to go through the time and expense of mediation as well as through the time and expense of a trial.

Working in the Children's Best Interests Using Collaborative Law

Collaborative law is a voluntary process that individuals who are interested in finding a litigation-free, respectful, and hands-on solution to family law-related issues enter into.[5] Collaborative law is an emerging field that has gained statutory and legal recognition in several states. Indiana is currently allowing parties to file collaborative law cases only in certain courts in certain counties. The collaborative practice allows the divorcing parties to resolve disputes respectfully by agreement. These are no-court divorces, in which the parties can involve trained professionals such as life coaches, child specialists, mental health professionals, and financial advisors to help settle disputes. For example, I recently worked on a collaborative law case in which neither parent could agree on a new budget for the children's extracurricular activities. We sat down as a group with a financial advisor, laid out the activities and the schedule, and compromised. Both parents left knowing their voices were heard, they treated each other respectfully, and they left with a resolution in a short period of time. They even left agreeing *how* they would tell the children they were each going to participate in one less activity. Collaborative law encourages respectful communication, lowers antagonism, and eliminates hostility and high conflict. Of course, the parties must be willing to engage with each other in this manner for collaborative law to work.

If a client expresses an interest in engaging in collaborative law, the attorney must first meet with the client to discuss the desired outcome. The attorney then acts as a facilitator to begin the conversation between the two parties. Parents can save a substantial amount of time and money by taking time in the first or second meeting to write down their individual goals for their

[5] International Academy of Collaborative Professionals, http://www.collaborativepractice.com (last visited Jul. 12, 2013).

children and their finances. The parties and their attorneys can then review the goals together and create a list of shared goals. It is relatively easy and fast to identify the couple's shared goals, allowing both parties to see that they still have certain objectives in common. This changes the parents' attitudes, outlook, and the way they treat each other. It also improves the nature of their communication. Collaborative law is a hugely successful way to practice law, and although it allows the parties more of a voice and more control in the process, it does not eliminate the need for attorneys (as the critics suggest). Attorneys are vital to the process—we draft the pleadings and the papers, and advise our clients separately. In essence, collaborative law is a forced mediation by agreement without a mediator. Everyone simply agrees to respectfully communicate their goals for their children and reach good decisions in the children's best interests.

Conclusion

Mothers and fathers are heading further toward equal ground when it comes to which parent is to have custody of their children. Historically, women and children were considered property and custody of children was given to fathers. Later on, it was assumed that a child belonged with their mother during his or her "tender years." Now, because divorces and separations are becoming more common, it is not uncommon for fathers to be just as likely to receive primary custody of the children. Yet some may still argue that although the "tender years" doctrine has essentially been abolished, courts across the country still greatly give preference to the mother in custody cases. However, despite this trend, the main focus of courts in current custody disputes is the best interest of the children. This has created a need to develop tools that are supposed to determine what is in the best interest of the children such as custody evaluations and child psychologists.

Collaborative practice and joint custody are incredibly important in preserving the health and continuity in relationships between parents and children. Many factors affect the child custody cases that go before judges; attorneys ask numerous questions and compile hundreds of factors that influence each case. Ultimately, however, it is most important to recognize the critical nature of a child having access to both parents. Shared parenting and joint childrearing are absolutely the best things we can do for children in a divisive family. Methods such as collaborative law allow us to place our focus in the right areas.

Key Takeaways

- Make nurturing, predictability, stability, and lack of disruption for a young child the main priorities in a parenting arrangement. Children under the age of five should have more frequent parental visits (versus longer visits) to fit the children's limited attention spans.
- Be able to consider both sides of a custody dispute, and if all is relatively equal, create a shared parenting and shared custody arrangement that is satisfactory to everyone. Involve a child-based expert in the process to ensure the children's best interests are a priority in your plan.
- Consider mediation as a favored method of dispute resolution. It may reduce the children's involvement in the process to a short conversation, instead of requiring them to go to a psychologist's office and testify at court as witnesses.
- If your jurisdiction allows it and your client is open to it, suggest using collaborative law in a divorce. It encourages respectful communication, lowers antagonism, and eliminates hostility and high conflict.

Gloria Mitchell is the owner of Mitchell Law Group, a northside Indianapolis-based law firm, with four full-time associates and a skilled support staff. Since 1988, she has practiced in the areas of domestic and family law litigation and mediation. Ms. Mitchell previously served as Master Commissioner in the Marion Superior Court, domestic division, and is a frequent speaker for various professional groups relating to a variety of topics with a focus on family law-related issues. Ms. Mitchell is trained in collaborative law and conflict resolution in high-conflict divorce cases. She received her BA degree from Miami University and her JD degree from Indiana University.

Ms. Mitchell is a member of the Indianapolis and Hamilton County Bar Associations, is a fellow and director of the Indianapolis Bar Foundation, named in Best Lawyers in America, and has been annually awarded recognition as a Super Lawyer by Indianapolis Monthly since 2007. Ms. Mitchell enjoys volunteering her time and legal expertise to the community through domestic violence and shelter counseling, Bar Association legal lines, and assisting not-for-profit corporations in securing corporate and tax status.

Acknowledgment: *The author would like to thank Ashley Balicki, Esquire, and Bailey Box, both of Mitchell Law Group, for their hard work and continued support.*

Teaching Clients to Be Their Own Advocates in Child Custody Cases

Andrew A. Zashin

Partner

Zashin & Rich Co. LPA

ASPATORE

Introduction

Child custody matters impact the most important facets of a client's life—their child and their relationship with their child. As a result, it is a stressful and emotional area of litigation with high stakes. In addition, a client's parenting decisions are intensely personal; having that parent-child relationship and those decisions examined under a proverbial microscope in litigation is difficult.

This chapter will help practitioners guide their clients through this difficult process and instruct them on how to present themselves in the best light possible. Specifically, the chapter includes tips on focusing the client on presenting relevant information in a concise way that substantiates his/her viewpoint to the court to a third-party evaluator. The chapter also discusses strategy concerning how to frame a custody litigation matter and when to engage (and when not to engage) a third-party expert. Most importantly, this chapter will focus the practitioner on the bigger—and often subjective—picture, emphasizing the importance of identifying the client's goals and managing the client's expectations in each phase of the process. Doing these things at the outset and reevaluating these points throughout the case allows the practitioner and the client to craft their definition of "success" based on the facts and circumstances of that individual matter.

Identifying Goals and Motivation in a Child Custody Case

When initiating a child custody case, it is most important to first identify the client's goals and evaluate whether those goals are realistic under the circumstances. Clients frequently create goals that simply are not attainable, and the lawyer must educate the client about what is likely to happen in court. If the client is not a smart consumer of legal services, and does not understand the probable results, the client is likely to be disappointed with the outcome. A realist, who is either naturally in tune with realistic outcomes or listens to a lawyer with an understanding of what will happen in court, is more likely to be satisfied with the outcome than an optimist who is certain of his or her case and is convinced the court will find in his or her favor. Realists know the outcome will not be perfect, but are mentally capable of accepting that fact.

Divorce lawyers are often viewed as counselors, and while many may cringe at the thought of being psychological therapists, it is true at times that they must be able to identify their clients' motivations to help make sense of the situation. For example, a client may want to keep a child away from a person the other parent is dating, but the lawyer realistically has a limited ability to do that in the absence of an overriding concern such as a safety issue or substance abuse. If the client simply is not accepting of the person's lifestyle, background, or religion, the lawyer cannot do much to help the client in that respect, and must be able to communicate this to the client. Understanding the client's motivation is important regardless of whether the client is in a pre-decree situation, or if a separation, divorce, or allocation of parental rights or responsibilities has already occurred. If the case is pre-decree, the court will determine what is in the children's best interest; if it is post-decree, the court will require the parties to demonstrate how the situation has changed, and why the parties are back in court. Many states have no-fault provisions, meaning people do not need grounds to get divorced. When fighting for child custody rights in a post-decree situation, however, people must have grounds in the form of a change of circumstance that affects the children's best interests. The change of circumstances must be significant in the court's opinion. Clients sometimes do not understand what is relevant, and lawyers often become fatigued wading through claims that are not valuable to the case. It is not uncommon for an inexperienced lawyer to lose track of a claim that is useful in advancing the client's position because it has been watered down by irrelevant details. If the client lists fifteen issues, only three of those are likely to matter in the case. It is the lawyer's responsibility to evaluate and prioritize those issues to determine which will be most beneficial to the client's case.

Examples of issues that usually are relevant to a client's case include: quantifiable problems or changes in the child's educational environment (i.e., severe drop in grades, many absences/tardies, etc.); quantifiable changes or a failure to address the child's medical needs or mental health needs; serious concerns about the child's well-being or behavior raised by a reputable third party (i.e., child's counselor, etc.); a parent's criminal charges or convictions for crimes of violence, crimes against children, or crimes involving substance abuse; and issues that impact the parent's ability to parent the child (i.e., substance abuse problems, mental health issues that are not being properly addressed).

Examples of issues that often matter less to the client's case are: issues involving differences in parenting styles (i.e., one parent may believe that the other parent allows the child to watch "too much" television, but this is not objectively poor parenting); issues that do not have an impact on one's ability to parent or a direct impact on the child; and one parent's past "lack of interest" in parenting or prior "division of labor" between the parties (i.e., now that the parties have separated, that parent will get his/her opportunity to be a more "hands-on" parent).

Clients should remain focused on long-term goals, and not get lost fighting about individual issues. Custody cases are marathons, not sprints, and if the client thinks about the case in terms of the legal result of a particular hearing or how it will affect the next school year, the client is likely to get a bad result. Instead, the client should consider the arc of the case, the minority of the child, and what will be best for that child over time, which will lead to the client being more satisfied with the outcome. Sometimes (counterintuitively) it actually makes sense for the client to let the other parent get what he or she wants—picking battles is critically important in a child custody case. The client should understand that certain issues will not matter over time, and if the client searches for leverage all the time on every issue (especially child custody issues), it might inure to the client's benefit on paper, but produce a bad result in life. Sometimes custody determinations are too good to be true and cannot be enforced—the client has essentially won the battle but lost the war. A good lawyer can prevent that situation by helping the client identify what to give up, what to fight for, and what to leverage.

Helping Clients Advocate Their Own Cases

Child custody cases can be exceedingly difficult, and experienced custody lawyers sometimes collect data and build cases systematically to yield the best possible result for the client. Attorneys should focus their clients on substantiating the facts to be proven, and eliminating the "he said/she said" conflict. If, for example, the mother does not drop off the kids at school on time, school records are essential in proving this fact. Objective information is always beneficial, and it is often possible for clients to provide it. For this reason, clients should think about what they can do to get the results they want, and what objective materials exist to help them prove their claims.

The types of documents necessary in a child custody case depend on the reason for the custody action. Clients can be their own best advocates, and should not approach a lawyer without first conducting some preliminary organization and prioritizing to give the lawyer the best, most-refined product with which to work. Clients must carefully consider how to collect documents and information that will make their cases impregnable when demonstrating how they can provide a home in the children's best interests. In any case, the client must produce documents that substantiate the facts that he or she wants to prove, such as school records, medical records, police reports, and school reports. While affidavits may not be admissible in court, they can persuade third parties such as psychological evaluators or guardians *ad litem*.

Encouraging Realistic Client Expectations

In the context of child custody litigation, the idea of "success" requires a paradigm shift for high-achieving lawyers and result-oriented clients. Child custody litigation is not a zero-sum game; lawyers and their clients cannot look at a spreadsheet and see which parent did better, or weigh the amount of custody hours awarded to determine who won or lost. Instead, "success" may be a matter of reaching a compromise that allows a child to participate in extracurricular activities, or may be measured in terms of the child's psychological comfort and the ease with which the child moves between the father and mother. The lawyer must outline this idea of success for the client from the outset so the client can form a realistic expectation for the case's outcome.

If the client meets the lawyer expecting to eliminate the other spouse's parental rights, the client will probably be disappointed. It is important for the client to understand that child custody decisions are made in courts of equity, not courts of law. No jury sits there; no one is ever right or wrong. The decisions rendered in domestic relations courts and family law courts are equitable decisions, and a significant amount of subjectivity imbues the outcomes. The statutes that guide family law courts contain a variety of factors determining spousal support and allocating parental rights and responsibilities. While these appear to be solid standards that people can satisfy objectively, in reality, as these cases unfold they involve more art than science, necessitating the lawyer to understand the subjective nature of the system and the predilections of the particular hearing officer.

Preparing a Client for Co-Parenting

Co-parenting arrangements are essential to achieving success in child custody cases. Both parents should not only be involved in the child's life, but should also be cooperative and able to share in making decisions and taking responsibility for the child. The courts are loathe to allow a situation to happen in which one parent makes all of the decisions and, except in unusual cases, seek balance between the parents. For this reason, if a client initiates a meeting with a lawyer by saying he or she has nothing to do with the other parent, or communicates with the other parent only through the children, the lawyer must convince the client of the importance of improving that communication. Co-parenting requires the parents to communicate in a spirit that is in the best interest of the children, not aimed at hurting the other spouse.

Advising Clients to Reconcile Issues from the Past

To get the desired results in court, the attorney must determine in advance how the client will address any challenges associated with issues from the client's past. The attorney should also discuss with the client any issues from the other parent's past. To avoid any surprises in court, the client should be forthcoming as the lawyer explores the situation and identifies the strengths and weaknesses in the client's case. The lawyer must be comfortable asking the client about the worst things he or she has ever done, including substance and domestic abuse. It is, of course, essential for the lawyer to know what the opposition will claim in court. If the client has made any parenting mistakes, the lawyer must be able to explain those mistakes, reconcile them, and explain how the client intends to handle the situation in the future. Clients must be able to package and produce their version of the facts instead of denying the problem or claiming it was not as bad as the opposition claims. Courts involved in custody issues have a tendency to forgive—it is the lawyer's and client's job to help the court believe it is in the children's best interest to be with that parent.

Preparing the Client for Court

It is important for clients to understand what to expect from the child custody litigation process. Too often, litigants expect an immediate trial and result, which, of course, are rare. In some places, the timeline for child custody cases is condensed, but for some time in one county in Ohio, pre-decree actions involving child custody concerns lasted well over two years (despite Supreme Court guidelines to the contrary). Those courts currently are much better at keeping to the eighteen-month guideline for child custody decisions, and other counties often are able to resolve cases within a year.

It is also important for the lawyer to educate the client about what to expect at particular hearings and legal junctures during the child custody litigation process. A client who has a sense of what to expect naturally feels better about the process as it proceeds. This also helps the lawyer and client prepare the necessary documents and proposals they plan to present, which should be done well in advance of going to court. Just as it is awful for a litigant to encounter surprise documents or plans from the opposition, it is not comfortable for a client if his or her own lawyer does the same. Everyone should know what is expected of him or her in terms of a particular court hearing. If the hearing involves talking about a temporary possession plan, for example, the client should see the proposal in advance, having reviewed and discussed it with the lawyer before the hearing. This helps get a more realistic result, which in turn creates a more satisfied client.

Just as clients should know what to expect from the child custody litigation process, they must also know what is expected of them. Clients should know when to speak, and how to be generally appropriate in court, including what to wear and what not to wear. A little common sense from the litigant goes a long way, but it is beneficial for the lawyer to provide additional guidance regarding what will be expected of the client.

Involving Third Parties in a Child Custody Case

It is sometimes beneficial to involve third parties, including mediators, guardians *ad litem*, and forensic psychologists, to help obtain the desired results in a child custody case. Experts play an especially pivotal role in cases where relocation is an issue, as relocation can lead to children suffering when broken away from their social networks, and mental health issues and issues of substance abuse and physical abuse occur with frightening frequency in these cases. Experts can help children in crisis, and an effective lawyer knows when to involve them. By bringing in an expert to testify for the client, the lawyer may be able to make a better argument to the court and get a better result for the client.

In today's society, where divorce is prevalent, one of the biggest challenges in divorce law is misinformation. Clients frequently get bad advice from friends they consider reliable; unfortunately, even the most well-intentioned friends (and sometimes lawyers) prove to be unreliable sources of information. Every child custody case is unique and varies in complexity; as such, clients should resist trusting information derived from family and acquaintances. Every family's circumstances are different, and a lawyer should be able to sense the uniqueness and character of each particular case. It is important for clients to understand what options truly exist, and these options *sometimes* involve a third party—it is as necessary for a client to be open-minded about hiring a psychiatrist, for example, as it is for the client to understand when hiring a third party is likely to backfire. If the lawyer believes the client will not present well—especially if the client is unwilling to follow the lawyer's lead—it might be best to avoid using experts.

It's most beneficial to involve a third party when the dispute is bigger than simply restructuring the family; sometimes, a third party with special skills or expertise can help to sort through deeper issues being alleged by one or both of the parents. A guardian *ad litem* may be beneficial when there is controversy over the child's wishes concerning custody (and whether those wishes are expressed in a mature way consistent with his/her best interest) or when there are factual disputes about each party's relationship with the child or impact on the child. A forensic psychologist may be helpful in a case where psychological/mental health issues or substance abuse issues are alleged, allegedly impact a party's ability to parent, or negatively impact the child. Finally, a mediator may be the appropriate choice in a case where the parties are not diametrically opposed to the other's position but need help working out the details of a parenting plan—often because they have a difficult time communicating with one another or developing creative alternatives that meet both their needs.

Involving a third party is likely to backfire when your client will not present well or will not follow your advice. One example is when you believe that your client is withholding information or being dishonest (either with you, with the third party or both); especially in cases where a guardian *ad litem* or forensic psychologist is involved, this behavior will speak volumes about your client's character and credibility. A third party will be less likely to believe your client's version of the facts and more likely to believe the potentially damaging things said by the other party about your client. Engaging a third party is also problematic when your client does not show insight into the current parenting situation or relationship dynamic. A client lacking insight—either because he/she is overwhelmed by negative emotions (such as anger at the other parent) or because he/she is unable to acknowledge his/her own contributions to the flawed parenting relationship—will often be viewed as a parent who is oblivious to the best interest of his/her child. Finally, some clients will refuse to cooperate with the third party. In those situations, it is best to avoid involving one at all, since the court will often interpret your client's refusal or reluctance to cooperate as a sign that your client is unreasonable.

When hiring experts, it is critical to define their roles. The client should understand how experts work; even if the client thinks the child therapist is on his or her side, a treating therapist may not be able to get involved in the case, or may want to maintain the professional therapeutic relationship outside of court. Even if the therapist testifies, he or she may be able to testify only to the facts at issue, address compliance or non-compliance, substantiate a diagnosis, or administer and interpret a test. In contrast, a forensic expert hired by the court can make an opinion, gather facts, and interview different parties. The forensic expert works with the goal of helping the court make a determination that makes sense under a particular scheme, whether it is a best-interest determination or a change-of-circumstances determination.

Similarly, sometimes people go to mediation and expect the mediator's result to be dispositive of an issue or a set of issues, but that is not what mediators do. It is important for the lawyer to stress to the client that mediators make recommendations after hearing both sides, and people are not necessarily bound by them. Often, people go through mediation and are disappointed when they find the result cannot be enforced and they must still go to court. Similarly, many people believe guardians *ad litem* will testify for one side, but their job is generally to be the representative, legal and otherwise, of the ward. They represent the child without picking a side, and how the case takes shape depends on the particular guardian's style. Because different experts work with different goals in mind, the lawyer must understand their various roles and how to use them to the client's benefit, or avoid using them to the case's detriment.

The lawyer should not only know how to effectively utilize experts, but also how to choose the right person to fit the circumstances. Some experts are sympathetic to certain issues and tend to dismiss others, so the attorney must know the expert well enough to predict whether that expert can help further the client's case. Many lawyers repeatedly use the same experts, which is not necessarily the best approach. It is often more helpful to bypass the local expert or an expert familiar to the court and instead use experts who have written books, identified syndromes, or worked on particular research. The client should not settle for a lawyer who does not have a network of people on whom to rely and substantial experience handling unique cases.

The lawyer must ensure the client provides relevant materials to the expert, without overloading the expert with unnecessary documents. Clients sometimes expect the expert to read every page of the materials they submit; instead, they should prioritize the materials with some guidance from the lawyer in determining the most important set of items or facts to consider.

The client should provide the third party with documents that are relevant to the issues in the case. If the case hinges on the child's educational needs, for example, the client should compile relevant school records concerning grades or absences or correspondence from teachers or administrators that speak directly to the issues in dispute. If the case concerns the health of the child or parents, medical records or mental health records should be provided and, if necessary, the client should sign releases allowing the third party to speak directly with treating medical or mental health care professionals. In a case involving criminal charges, police reports, criminal court dockets or probation records should be obtained and presented. If substance abuse issues are involved, any substance abuse treatment records or drug or alcohol testing results or assessments should be reviewed by the third party. In cases where a mediator is trying to assist the parties with fashioning a parenting time schedule, it may be helpful to bring school calendars, work schedules, etc., to allow everyone to work with concrete dates and times.

Conclusion

The difficult and emotional word of child custody litigation requires an attorney to utilize a broad range of skills to teach his/her client how to be his/her own best advocate. The attorney has to focus (and often re-focus) the client on probable outcomes and on what components of those outcomes are really important to the client and to the client's relationship with his/her child. The attorney has to strategize with the client about short-term and long-term goals; putting together this strategy requires complete disclosure on the part of the client and frank discussions about personal topics to avoid surprises. Finally, the attorney assists the client with presenting relevant evidence and with navigating the involvement of any third-party expert in the case.

To be successful as a family law attorney in custody matters, an attorney should be honest, compassionate, insightful, creative/open-minded, and have "thick skin." A client's interest is better served by an attorney who keeps the client on an informed and realistic path than an attorney who tells the client what he/she wants to hear. Similarly, a client can greatly benefit from an attorney who looks for creative solutions to disputes instead of an attorney who believes that "one size fits all." In custody litigation, even the most likable clients are engaged in a highly emotional and stressful situation; as a result, the client is likely to lash out at his/her attorney at some point in the process. An attorney new to this practice area should seek out a mentor and/or colleagues to brainstorm and consult with on custody litigation issues. Drawing from the experience of other respected practitioners will help an attorney new to custody litigation develop the necessary skills for success.

Key Takeaways

- When initiating a child custody case, first identify the client's goals and evaluate whether those goals are realistic under the circumstances. If the client is not a smart consumer of legal services, and does not understand the probable results, the client is likely to be disappointed with the outcome.
- Focus your clients on substantiating the facts to be proven and eliminating the "he said/she said" conflict. Objective information is always beneficial, and it is often possible for clients to provide it. For this reason, ask your clients to think about what they can do to get the results they want, and what objective materials exist to help them prove their claims.
- Understand that child custody litigation is not a zero-sum game; you cannot look at a spreadsheet and see which parent did better, or weigh the amount of custody hours awarded to determine who won or lost. Instead, "success" may be measured in terms of the child's psychological comfort and the ease with which the child moves between the father and mother. Outline this idea of success for the client from the outset so the client can form a realistic expectation for the case's outcome.
- Educate the client about what to expect at particular hearings and legal junctures during the child custody litigation process. A client who has a sense of what to expect naturally feels better about the process as it proceeds.
- Because different experts work with different goals in mind, ensure you understand their various roles and how to use them to the client's benefit or avoid using them to the case's detriment.

Andrew A. Zashin is a partner of the Ohio law firm Zashin & Rich Co. LPA which is headquartered in Cleveland, Ohio. Mr. Zashin represents high-net worth individuals and others with complex divorce and child custody cases throughout Ohio, nationally and internationally. He is licensed in Ohio, New York, Florida, Washington, DC, and the United States Federal Court.

Mr. Zashin is an adjunct professor of law at Case Western Reserve University's School of Law where he teaches the Advanced Family Law course every year. He is the recipient of many honors and awards and was recently named the "Lawyer of the Year" (2013, Cleveland metropolitan area) in the nation's premier legal rating guide "Best Lawyers." In 2007, Worth Magazine (Robb Report) named Mr. Zashin to its list of the "Top 100" attorneys in the nation. He is also named in the elite lawyers rating guide "Best Lawyers in America," has an "AV" Martindale-Hubbell rating, and has been selected as an "Ohio Super Lawyer" since the magazine was first published in Ohio. He is a fellow of The American Academy of Matrimonial Lawyers and of the International Academy of Matrimonial Lawyers and routinely represents individuals with interests outside of the United States.

Working with Your Client Toward a Successful Child Custody Case

Gavin K. Doi

Partner

Doi/Luke, Attorneys at Law LLLC

Introduction

Successful child custody cases have a common thread running through them—they require effective communication between attorney and client. More so than other types of cases, working in close conjunction with the client is a necessity. Communication with the client not only provides the attorney with the factual background to successfully litigate a custody case, but equally importantly it allows the attorney to determine what constitutes a successful result for the client. What we as attorneys may see as a success may differ significantly from what the clients have envisioned for themselves as a happy resolution.

This chapter discusses what the experienced custody attorney should be seeking in communication with their client: understanding the best interests of the child; specific concerns in the areas of paternity, domestic abuse, and international custody; and strategies for working with the client toward a successful resolution.

Each child custody case is individual and unique. Attorneys handling these cases, particularly after years of practice, must avoid the trap of simply pigeonholing cases and being too formulaic in their approach. To be a successful child custody lawyer, that lawyer must understand their client.

Best Interests of the Child

The Best Interests of the Child standard needs to be fully explained to clients, particularly because many clients do not understand that "Best Interests of the Child" is not necessarily equal to "fair." This creates the need to assess cases objectively, as what a client wants may be different from the child's best interests. As an example a client may seek an equal timesharing arrangement where their young child is exchanged on a week-to-week basis, whereas that type of long stretch between exchanges is often viewed as difficult for younger children. Conversely a parent may want to exchange the child very frequently during the week, in a manner that disrupts the child's ability to settle in any one place.

Often in child custody disputes, clients will see custody as a zero-sum game or as a battle where each "loss" upsets or angers them. Each issue or point becomes “won” or “lost,” and this often causes the parents to lose sight of the best interests of the child, causing the parents to make emotionally charged decisions. They fail to see the long-term consequences of seeking to limit the other parent’s involvement with the child.

Parents can become caught up in the numbers game of custody timesharing, where the loss or gain of a day each month becomes an object of fixation. This type of custody accounting can easily cause parents to lose sight of the child’s best interests. Some parents have the urge to lobby their children, or sway them to their side. This type of parental alienation is not only harmful, but can be very damaging to their own custody case.

Attorneys can help clients avoid these pitfalls by counseling them about the courts’ belief that children need both parents’ involvement in their lives. Further, attorneys should advise the client that the courts are currently much more receptive to joint custody, both legal and physical, than in the past.

Although it is sometimes difficult, the custody attorney needs to set aside time for each overwrought or emotional client, and discuss with them the bigger picture and help them refocus.

It is important to try to get clients away from over-focusing on the count of days in timesharing, and to instead focus on what the child really needs, as well as what they themselves truly need. For example, some parents, feeling that they are being slighted in custody or visitation, will take up the mantra of joint custody: “I need joint custody,” or “I will only accept joint custody.” In reality, some of these parents are not actually prepared for the practicalities of joint custody.

Attorneys should discuss with clients that by lobbying their children, they are causing distress to them and should advise them that such lobbying may backfire on them with a guardian *ad litem* or custody evaluator.

Paternity Issues

Occurring more frequently have been divorces in which the husband is discovered to not be the father of a child born during the marriage. This type of development has come in two varieties: (1) instances in which the husband had believed himself to be the biological father of the child, until subsequent revelation; and (2) instances in which the husband was already aware that he was not the biological father, but held himself out as such.

Situations in the first model typically result in fights over whether or not the presumption of husband being the biological parent should be rebutted. Those cases in the second model focus on whether or not the husband should continue to be the legal father, having been the "psychological father" of the child in question.

Establishing Parentage

Proceeding formally, things are as they have been in the past where individuals seeking to have parentage established need to file petitions for paternity. In many states, however, fathers who execute form affidavits at the time of the child's birth are considered to be legally established as the father of that child. In such cases, petitions for paternity are not needed, but such individuals may file a petition for custody, visitation, and support, which ask the court to make orders regarding the child.

Decreasing costs in technology have generated more options. "Home" DNA paternity tests are significantly more accessible. In many instances, individuals do not actually need a court-facilitated DNA test, but simply want to verify parentage for their own peace of mind. Such tests only require the DNA sample from the child and one parent. Then the samples can be sent by mail to testing laboratories. DNA results are generated a short time later. The expense for these tests has been lessened greatly by not including the "chain of custody" involving the lab that draws the samples.

Benefits for Children in Establishing Paternity

The establishment of parentage can result in a number of significant benefits to children.

Among them:

- *Establishment of custody and visitation orders.* As part of a paternity petition, the court will issue orders regarding the child's custody and visitation. Even in situations where the parents have been cooperating up to that point, it can be very beneficial to have orders to fall back upon when the parents are in disagreement.

- *Increased likelihood of child support being paid.* The establishment of child support automatically follows the establishment of paternity; further, the establishment of parentage may inspire the noncustodial parent to financially contribute to the child's care.
- *Increased likelihood of both parents being involved in raising of child.* As with child support, the establishment of parentage may "vest" the noncustodial parent to actively co-parent the child.
- *Laws of inheritance/intestacy.* With parentage established, the child may clearly and cleanly benefit from a state's intestacy law, in the event of the parent's death. In such instance, a typical state's intestacy law provides for a child's right of inheritance from a deceased parent's estate; lacking the establishment of paternity, the child may be blocked from such a claim. This is of particular note when observing parties attempting to establish paternity posthumously for such purpose.
- *Medical insurance benefits.* Parentage or other court orders will be required by most employers to extend medical insurance benefits to employees' children.
- *Other benefits.* As with medical insurance benefits, employers will require established parentage to apply other benefits, such as military privileges, to children of employees.

Strategies for Paternity Cases

Consultation. When meeting with the client and before filing, determine what the client is seeking (support, co-parenting, visitation, medical insurance). Determine what the existing living or care arrangements are for the child and the other parent's willingness and ability to care for the child. Ask about the other parent's living situation or care arrangements for the child. Based on the answers to these questions, consider the client's chances to obtain the sought-after custody result.

Preparing the filing. Once the initial assessments have been done, assess the timetable and if there is any urgency to filing. Urgency would relate to any pressing circumstances that the client may be facing. Examples of these types of circumstances include if the other parent is seeking to leave the jurisdiction with the child, or if the other parent presents a threat of imminent abuse to the child, either physical or emotional. If the circumstances warrant, a concurrent request to the court for an expedited hearing may be made. Bear in mind, however, that in such custody cases a significant number of parties seeking relief will also be seeking an expedited hearing, so the basis for your request needs to be compelling. When preparing a request to expedite or to shorten time for hearing, clearly lay out the facts that create the urgency for the hearing. Again, these types of requests to the judges are numerous, so try to illustrate the unique nature of the urgency. Client affidavit statements such as "I need to see my child now" will not suffice without something more.

In petitions without expediting requests, prepare the filing documents with the client while also gathering any necessary supporting documents, such as birth certificates (if available) and pay stubs (for financial statements). Additionally, documents that support the client's assertions should be gathered for use as exhibits. This type of evidence may include:

- Receipts or evidence of expenditures on behalf of the child, as credit toward past child support claims
- E-mail or texts between the parties
- Phone records (often easily obtainable through the client printing out online mobile phone statements)
- Facebook, Twitter, or other social media postings (recommend that if the client has access to such postings, that they should print them immediately due to the possibility that they may be removed at any time)
- Childcare or school documents that demonstrate participation of the client in the child's education, or conversely the exclusion of the client from such participation
- School report cards or progress reports

Between Filing and the Hearing. The client should be strongly advised regarding use of e-mail and mobile phone texts with the other parent, as well as any other parties connected to the other parent. Texts in particular are being treated by individuals like conversations, and people therefore tend to be less guarded in their statements than e-mail or written correspondence. Clients may issue damning statements to the other party, especially during heated exchanges. While you do not wish to cut off communication between the parents—which would stifle co-parenting—clients should be directed to keep to the facts in such communication with the other parent.

Social media, as noted earlier, has become an area of concern for all custody litigators. Both clients and opposing parties may have posted photos or comments that may be damaging to their positions or claims. It is a best practice to advise clients to significantly limit or even cease their social media posting during the litigation process. It has been shown many times that postings that are "private" carry no assurances. The most certain way for clients to avoid posting damaging material is to not post at all, although that may be unrealistic, depending on the client, so counsel them as best you can.

Complications in Paternity Cases

Often, paternity cases, unlike divorce cases, involve two parties who have had limited time living together or working toward resolving their disputes. Similarly, the parties often have very limited (or even no) experience together in co-parenting. Rather than dealing with a former couple that had made a specific commitment, you may be dealing with two people who had a brief relationship or virtually no relationship at all. This must be taken into account in crafting final settlements. A finished custody order in such situations will typically need language regarding the handling of holiday timesharing and third-party childcare. Whereas a former couple may have knowledge of how each celebrated occasions in the past, two parents who have little to no experience with each other may need more time and effort to craft a workable schedule.

Best Practices in Cases That Include Domestic Abuse

Even more than in other family cases, it is critical to truly listen to your client in cases where domestic abuse might be an issue. Bear in mind when working with domestic violence victims that it is important to listen without showing judgment. Many victims are already suffering from guilt or fear of having come so far as to seek legal help. Domestic violence prevention groups often note that a victim may attempt to leave their abuser several times before actually successfully doing so.

Domestic abuse cases involving children as direct victims or as witnesses to abuse of other family members call for the use of counselors or social workers (collectively referred to herein as "therapists") to explore the impact on the children. Communication with the therapist yields critical information for the custody case. When therapists are reluctant to discuss the child's issues with the attorneys, or are averse to being brought into the related litigation, typically a guardian *ad litem* or a custody evaluator can bridge the gap. This allows the therapist to convey concerns to the court without impairing the therapist-patient relationship with the child.

Although it should apply to all cases, complete candor from the client becomes paramount. In a sense, the role of a family lawyer can be similar to the role of a criminal defense lawyer in that the family lawyer cannot adequately address and prepare for a custody dispute without having a clear understanding of what happened. Once a firm grasp of the factual situation is gained, assess whether the alleged abuse is one of a recurring nature or an isolated incident. Obviously, abuse that can be effectively conveyed to the court as the latter type is more containable and more manageable for the client's case. In presenting to the court, it is important to convey your client's candidness regarding the alleged conduct. If the client is admitting to the conduct, the focus should be on the client's recognition of the damaging nature of the conduct, and equally upon the steps the client has taken to address it.

Best Practices When the Custodial Parent Lives in Another Country

Initially, try to gather evidence from the client regarding the child's country of residence, whether it is the United States or a foreign country. A family lawyer needs to make an honest assessment of the evidence for both countries' claims. If it is determined that the United States was the country of habitual residence for the child but now the child has been taken to another country by the other parent, the family lawyer must turn to the Hague Convention on the Civil

Aspects of International Child Abduction (Hague Convention), and specifically whether or not the other country in this scenario is a signatory to the Hague Convention. A similar analysis must be used if the lawyer determines that another country was the country of habitual residence for the child, but the child is now present in the United States.

The signatory status for the Hague Convention is a substantial issue in Hawaii, where a significant portion of the population are immigrants from Asia, and much of Asia including Japan and the Philippines have not signed the Convention. (At the time of this writing, Japan's legislature is completing the final steps toward ratification.)

Strategies for Successfully Litigating Child Custody Cases

Client-Attorney Relationship

In an effective family law attorney-client relationship, clients should clearly and honestly present their factual situation, realistically and reasonably establish their goals in custody, and try to make decisions that are in the best interests of their child as well as what is truly in their own best interests, and to avoid making decisions made in furtherance of spite, or upon principle alone.

Practices vary depending on the demographics of the client (e.g., gender, ethnicity, age, sexual orientation, socioeconomic status, etc.). If clients are very young, we often involve their parents in the process to a limited extent if the young parent is looking to his or her parent for direction; if the client is living with the parents, either temporarily or long term; or if the grandparents provide some of the care for the child (daycare, afterschool care, etc.)

Initial Client Meeting

In a family law consult, I begin by asking clients to lay out their factual situations, fully and completely. At that time, I allow them to present without interjecting my own opinions or strategic ideas, but the following should be addressed by the client during this time:

- Ages and conditions of the child(ren)
- Prior care arrangements of the child(ren), pre-breakup

- Current care arrangements of the child(ren), since the breakup
- Cause(s) of the parties' breakup

Thereafter, the clients should discuss what they are seeking regarding custody. Following that is the more appropriate time for me to share with the client my observations regarding what has happened so far, as well as my thoughts on strategy. Finally, at this point, the client likely has a number of burning questions that should be addressed. These questions usually focus on what will happen going forward, what the "odds" are of reaching their goals, how much time the process will take, and how much it will cost.

All of these are understandable concerns, and should hopefully be addressed in the initial meeting.

Essential Components to Building a Sound Case

A sound custody case requires framing the client as the primary caretaker of the child. This demonstrates to the court that placing the child with the client serves the best interests of the child.

It is important to outline that the client has a sound and thoughtful parenting plan, thus assuring the court that if it makes an award of custody for the client, it has a workable and realistic basis.

Finally, it is essential to demonstrate that under the client's parenting plan, the other parent will have a role in the child's life. This addresses the judicial system's position that both parents need to play a significant part in a child's life.

Understandably, these steps differ in cases where abuse or parental alienation has been involved. In both instances, the parenting plan may involve a more limited role for the parent who has engaged in the detrimental behavior, for the good of the child. An example of this would be supervised visitation, either for the child's physical protection or for monitoring how the supervised parent is communicating with the child.

Addressing Client Misconceptions

A common misconception in child custody cases is the frequent idea that "fathers have no chance" or that "mothers always win," or that "judges are biased in favor of moms." Toward this idea, I outline the court's use of the Best Interests of the Child standard and further how the court is looking to determine who has been the child's primary caretaker. I try to outline to clients the fact that more frequently the mothers tend to be the primary caretakers of the children prior to a split, and thus under the Best Interests of the Child standard the mother will similarly emerge more frequently with physical custody.

A common misconception is that simply terming a custody arrangement "joint" ends the discussion. Clients need to understand that joint physical custody involves more or less equal timesharing of the children, rather than joint in name only.

Another frequent misconception is the idea that if the other parent has legal and physical custody, then the other parent has "nothing." It is important to stress with them that they continue to maintain their rights of parentage, visitation rights, rights to information regarding the child, as well as the ongoing possibilities in changing custody.

Supporting Clients

Attorneys can support clients in the following ways:

- Clearly and fully understanding the factual background of the custody situation.
- Educating the client on how custody is determined by the court.
- Defining with the client a clear set of goals in custody.
- Preparing the client's expectations by outlining the best and worst-case scenarios.
- Ensuring that the clients realistically understand the procedural process and time involved.

Opening a Child Custody Case

Credible Grounds for Starting a Case

A child custody case should be initiated when the opposing party parent is unreasonable or unrealistic about the custody situation, and thus unwilling to amicably resolve the matter. A case should also be started if the other parent is acting abusively or negligently toward the child.

Information and Documents Needed for a Child Custody Case

Most of the information that the clients need is already in the clients' heads, by personal knowledge. Custody attorneys need clients to provide information on other subjects such as the child's upbringing, care arrangements, parenting concerns for either parent, and time constraints of both parents (work schedules, availability, etc.).

Among those documents helpful to a custody case are the child's school or childcare records; the child's recent medical records; if kept, the client's journal or log regarding parenting or timesharing (if this has not been kept, I typically request that the client begin keeping such a log); any records regarding related court cases (temporary restraining orders, criminal cases, child protective services investigations); and pay statements, W-2 forms, and tax returns, as they will be necessary for child support.

Preparing Clients for Court

Attorneys should set realistic and credible expectations for court appearances. Often, clients do not have a clear understanding of the sometime drawn-out timeframe of custody cases. Despite reviewing the steps and process of the case with the client repeatedly, at an initial hearing the client will sometimes ask, "So, after this hearing, will we be divorced?" In these instances, we need to outline the process again, so that clients can get a clear picture of how long this type of case may take. Similarly, it needs to be explained that at these non-final hearings (such as in motions for temporary custody) the results obtained, either favorable or unfavorable, are only temporary ones. It is important that clients do not feel that each hearing is a final showdown of some sorts. Clients also need to understand the logistics of the court process. Often, the court calendar on a hearing date is crowded with other cases, and judges may have limited time for the presentation of each case. As such, clients also need to understand that in addition to the substance of their evidence, the organization and conciseness are extremely important.

Alternative Dispute Resolution in Child Custody Cases

Two types of Alternative Dispute Resolution (ADR) that can be effective in child custody cases are mediation and parent counseling or parent coordination. All types of ADR place even more importance upon client communication than usual, as the client will have an even more hands-on role in the process as compared to litigation.

The mediation process is often only as strong as the mediator, because mediating a custody case involves a fine balance of high-conflict parties with flaring emotions. Often, judges will cite the strength of mediation as allowing the parties to reach a resolution of their own creation rather than one handed down by the court. Among the primary strengths of mediation is the ability for the parties to work together toward a resolution without sitting in a room face to face. Because the emotional level is so high, mediating by shuttle diplomacy can often serve to keep the peace. In any event, mediation increases the possibility that each party will be able to hear out the other party's concerns, which often gets blocked out in court.

One of the weaknesses of mediation stems from a power imbalance between the parties, either real or perceived. If one party feels it holds the cards in a mediation, it will not feel the real impetus to compromise. Similarly, if both parties do not attempt to mediate in good faith, it is rare that a resolution can be reached. Such situations can leave the client angry and frustrated.

Working with a therapist trained in effective parent counseling can be very successful, as it allows the parties a great deal of time and space to lay out their thoughts and concerns, and hopefully generate a better ability to understand the perspective of the other parent. The nature of this process usually involves more groundwork to be laid than in the mediation process. The parent counselor will take time to educate the parents in the co-parenting process as well as in understanding the positions of the other parent.

The client must be open to working in conjunction to resolve the dispute through ADR. If clients do not buy in to the idea of cooperation and compromise, any kind of meaningful settlement is unlikely. The process is significantly enhanced where both parties enter into ADR with the idea that reaching an agreement is truly best for the child.

Such a process usually involves a greater "speaking role" for the client, as he or she will be asked to articulate thoughts, positions, and concerns about custody. This can be difficult for many individuals.

Successful Settlement Outcomes

Successful outcomes of cases are situations where my clients receive custody arrangements that they are happy with, yet the other parties are not left seething nor are they left emotionally destitute. Although the "defeat" of the other party in such a situation may have the initial look of success, it too often leaves little possibility for effective co-parenting in the future. Further, it sometimes creates serious harm for the child, as the parent left with the lesser role may simply stop trying in his or her parenting efforts. A better result does not unnecessarily antagonize nor demoralize the other parent, leaving open the door for successful co-parenting. Further, an opposing party who is angry and upset over the custody result tends to cultivate an ongoing custody war, which will continue to be waged on the post-decree/judgment calendars of the court. This could hardly be confused with a rousing success. A successful outcome would be one that gives your client more or less the type of custodial time and authority he or she was seeking, and leaves an opposing party that may not be necessarily happy but is not demoralized over the custody situation, and a child or children who will benefit from this balance.

I often tell my clients that winning the case is not the complete and utter victory over the other parent. It is obtaining a result where everyone is content with the custody and the co-parenting relationship is not destroyed. Otherwise, in the future, there will be celebrations for the child such as graduations and other events, and rather than enjoying those events, both parents will have a hard, tight feeling in their chests, grinding their teeth when they see each other. That is not winning. Part and parcel of winning is being happy.

Essential features of a custody case include maintenance of the lines of communication between parents, allowing for effective co-parenting. This kind of continuing communication may allow parents to avoid future litigation through discussion or alternative dispute resolution such as mediation or parent counseling.

Also essential is a time schedule that is not only what the client wants, but also is practicable and realistic. Often, clients have unrealistic physical custody goals where they want "all" the time, or "at least half," but their work and other obligations will not allow for such a schedule.

The key characteristic of a satisfactory child custody settlement relates back to the basis for custody: that the resolution needs to be in the best interests of the child. While this may seem to be simply aspirational language, it should be the focus of the settlement. Where most child professionals agree that the separated family has detrimental effects on a child, the parties must keep sight of the goal to minimize these effects.

Custody settlements need to be practical. Specifically, such resolutions need to be workable for parents and child, in time and in money. Reaching a settlement in which the client achieves their goal of the majority of the child's time, but seriously interferes with the client's ability to work, or causes the child to be left unattended for long periods of time, would hardly be viewed as a "success" in the larger picture.

A satisfactory custody settlement needs to allow both parents to have a meaningful part in the child's life. While "meaningful" is not necessarily equal to "joint," the chance that the child will be raised in a positive environment increases dramatically. Another measurement of success is that both parents have to some extent accepted the settlement. While they do not have to be thrilled about the outcome, it has to be a settlement with which they can live.

On the financial front, the successful child custody settlement must also incorporate the child support issue. One can rarely find a child support dollar figure with which both parents are happy, as it will always be "too high" for one parent or "too low" for the other. Nonetheless, a number with which both parents can reasonably live is very important for long-term success of the custody settlement. An overly burdensome child support payment (for the payor) or an excessively sparse payment (for the payee) will create future stress upon the settlement, where the unhappy parent will eventually seek to change the custody situation so as to adjust the child support. A settlement with a workable number is very important.

Child Custody Litigation Challenges and Advice

The most common challenge in litigating custody is acknowledging clients' emotional concerns while simultaneously focusing clients on the litigation. It is important to break the case down into manageable pieces. If you have partners, associates, or a capable staff, delegating out portions of the case can make the core issues easier to deal with.

Best practices are learned through trial and error. I learn through not only my own attempts, but in complex cases I pay attention to the opposing counsel's strategies and case management. This involves not only watching those I want to emulate for their approaches, but also watching the approaches of those attorneys whom I wish to avoid emulating. I try to observe the discrete issues and the approaches and results, as well as just the overall win or loss aspect of the case.

In the past, there was much less stress put on the idea that both parents had to be significantly involved in the child's life. As child therapists have successfully spread the idea that a child benefits greatly from meaningful involvement of both parents, this has changed the direction of family law practitioners and judges. This has naturally increased the number of cases where parents are sharing legal and/or physical custody, or have greater amounts of visitation for the noncustodial parent.

Conclusion

Working in concert with the client is essential to obtaining a successful child custody resolution. As such, a quality family lawyer's skill set includes the ability to clearly hear what the client is saying, as well as clearly explaining to the client what is needed and what to expect. In starting such a client-lawyer relationship, the lawyer's *giving* of legal information, guidelines, and reasonable expectations, and *taking* of factual information, background, and the client's goals, are of equal importance.

A quality family lawyer, whether in practice for three years or thirty, needs to be mindful of the importance of communicating with the client. Even as the laws and standards regarding child custody evolve and change, the need for effective two-way communication with the client remains the same.

Key Takeaways

- Establishing effective two-way communication with the client at the outset is critical to setting up a custody plan and expectations.
- Unlike divorce cases, paternity cases may involve two individuals who have not had a longstanding previous relationship. This must be taken into account when crafting settlements.
- When building a sound custody case, it is important to outline that the client has a sound and thoughtful parenting plan that is workable and realistic.
- Mediation can be very effective in resolving child custody cases. Often, judges will cite the strength of mediation as allowing the parties to reach a resolution of their own creation rather than one handed down by the court.
- A "win" in a child custody case is a custody arrangement with which everyone can live, and the co-parenting relationship is not destroyed.

Gavin K. Doi is a partner with Doi/Luke, Attorneys at Law LLC, in Honolulu, Hawaii, practicing primarily in the area of divorce and family law. He was born and reared in Honolulu, Hawaii, receiving his juris doctorate from University of Denver College of Law in Denver, Colorado and his bachelor of arts in political science from Reed College in Portland, Oregon. Previously, Mr. Doi worked with the Child Support Enforcement Agency and the SAVD Domestic Violence Clinic. In his spare time, he volunteers time with Volunteer Legal Services Hawaii and the Hawaii State Bar Association, and coaches high school mock trial students.

Mr. Doi is a member of the Hawaii State Bar Association and the HSBA Family Law Section, and was presented with the 2002 Justice Award by the Hawaii State Bar Association, which honors one lawyer annually for their outstanding contribution to the ideals of justice, and was recognized in 2012 by the Hawaii Access to Justice Commission for his outstanding pro bono service to the Hawaii community.

Child Custody: Modern Trends and Observations

Anne Lamkin Durward

Shareholder

Massey Stotser & Nichols PC

Introduction

Over the past several years, child custody and visitation issues have come into the forefront in the divorce arena. This chapter will address the changing trends and expectations of litigants in this realm. No longer is it "assumed" that the mother will get custody and that the father will be the "weekend" parent. As more women have entered the workforce, the household models have radically changed. In this economy, both parents work to support the family and their lifestyles. When a divorce comes into the picture, parents have to adjust their schedules, their expectations, and their ideas as to what is truly best for the children. Trends across the country have been to develop "parenting plans" that are far more extensive and detailed than ever before.

This chapter will also look at the impact of abuse in a custody situation and how to structure your case around allegations of abuse. Abuse can come in many forms: physical, verbal, and emotional. Abuse can also be abuse of narcotics, alcohol or other substances. Situations involving abuse can have dramatic and long-lasting effects on the children and as practitioners we have to be aware of those impacts while looking after our clients.

The "Tender Years Presumption" and Child Custody Litigation

For years, the courts operated under the "tender years" presumption that basically assumed that children should be placed with the mother because of their youth. Over time this presumption has been abolished, but the fact of the matter is that mothers seem to be favored over the fathers when the children are very young. Even experienced practitioners hesitate to separate an infant from his/her mother before the age of one for overnight visitations with the father. However, I have noticed that the prior limitation on a father's custodial time with a small child has been evolving. The courts have begun to recognize that fathers can take care of their small children as well as (or in some cases better than) the mothers. It is important to assess who has been the primary caregiver for the child prior to the divorce filing and how the parents have handled their parental duties and responsibilities. As more women have entered the workforce and men are helping out more at home, the opinions have shifted. No longer does the woman stay home and take care of the children. Now children are in daycare, and both parents care for the children. Generally, the fathers have embraced this change and are asking for more if not equal time with the children.

Joint Custody in Child Custody Litigation

Joint custody is still a fairly new trend, and some judges, lawyers, and litigants still resist the concept. Generally, if the parents can agree to set aside their differences and parent the children even after the divorce, then joint custody can work. However, if one parent consistently has to be in charge, manipulates situations, and wants to play the children off of the parent, then joint custody can be very difficult. It seems best to designate one of the parents as the primary physical custodian and to give "tiebreakers" for important decision-making authority. Tiebreakers typically include education, medical/dental treatment, sports, religion, civic, cultural, and the like. Tiebreakers allow one parent to make the final decision when they cannot agree. For example, if the mother, who has the "tiebreaker" for medical decisions, wants the child to have a nose job and the father does not agree that the child should have a nose job, the mother's decision is final and the child is having a nose job. Otherwise, without tiebreakers, it is no different than a corporation with 50/50 shareholders. Neither party can act until they both agree.

The key difference between types of custodial arrangements is the custodial times for the parents. In the beginning of this trend, the phrase was "joint custody," but the reality was no different. Typically, the father had the same standard visitation he would have had under a sole custody arrangement. Courts seem to be evolving to allow for more expansive custodial times, especially under joint custody agreements. Some judges feel that no parent should go more than a few days without seeing his or her child. While this trend is still in the beginning stages, it is becoming more prevalent or expected. Many courts now refer to these arrangements as "parenting time guidelines" or "parenting plans." Some courts start from the premise that the time will be divided equally between the parents and it is up to the litigants to show why the time should not be divided equally.

As a practical matter, if both sides can set aside their differences and co-parent, that is a wonderful result for the children. Unfortunately, the reality is often not the case and the equal custodial times can be detrimental to the children. This can happen when homework does not get done when they are with one parent, or they cannot participate in activities because one parent will not allow them to do so, or the parents simply cannot put aside their differences. The courts should look at each situation in crafting custodial awards rather than just trying to fit every case into the same mold.

"Best Interest of the Child" Standard

The best interest of the child standard applies in the initial divorce proceeding or when the parents have true joint custody with no designation of a primary physical custodian. To support the child's best interests, the court should review which parent provides the child with the best chance for stability and consistency, which parent will ensure needs are met, which parent has historically met those needs, and which parent can provide security and well-being for the child. These needs can be met in a variety of ways and support of these needs is demonstrated by what each parent has done while raising the child. Parents should not be "punished" because they worked while the other parent stayed at home. The court must review all factors involved to make the decision about what is truly best for the children.

Pitfalls in Child Custody Cases

Parties involved in a child custody case need to be aware of how the courts will perceive their actions with regard to their children. Pitfalls can come in many forms and shapes, and it is important as the practitioner to know your judges and what their concerns may be. Listed herein are many areas that can cause a judge to rule for you or against you in a custody matter.

Actions the court may not look favorably upon include deliberately overscheduling the child so the other parent's time is limited by the activities. By the same token, a parent's failure to make sure the child gets to practices and games may be perceived as a strike against that parent. It is a careful balancing act.

Courts do not like when one parent insists on being in control or in charge of the child and who discounts the involvement of the other parent. Failing to keep the other parent informed about activities, school performances, sporting events, and medical appointments can all have repercussions. With technology now, it is so easy for both parents to be added to the e-mail blasts from school, coaches, and other parents that there is really no excuse for both parents to not be kept informed as to the children and their school and activities.

Using the children to deliver messages from one parent to the other, and involving the children in visitation issues, or support issues, are also not looked upon favorably.

Parents involved in child custody battles frequently make the mistake of losing sight of what is important—their children. They get so focused on who is going to be in charge, who is going to win, or who is telling whom what to do that they forget that the children's health, well-being and security are what is important. Attorneys should be the rational people in the room. If you allow yourself to get caught up in the drama of the client, you lose your effectiveness and sometimes your credibility.

As attorneys, we are there to advise our clients, even when they do not want to hear the advice. For example, a mother is insisting that the father only have supervised visitation, if any. The evidence to support such restrictions does not exist, or the facts do not rise to that level. The mother wants to move forward with this as the only option for visitation. You have to advise your client on the law, how the judge will view the situation, and what your client's likelihood of success is. You also have to be willing to stand up to them and their demands. Your reputation and integrity have to be protected, because once lost, they will never be regained.

Paternity Issues

Many men do not realize that they can seek to establish paternity and ask for custody, support or visitation. I have filed several actions for men who have been cut off from the mothers of the children because the men were not the legal fathers and they had no rights on paper. Once we have filed the Complaint for Paternity and taken the DNA test to confirm the parentage, these cases are not much different than a typical child custody case.

In Alabama, paternity cases are filed in family court by the mother, the father, or by the Alabama Department of Human Resources. The court can award child support for up to two years prior to the filing of the complaint for paternity and child support or from the date of birth if it is less than two years. The court can also make an award for birth expenses that the mother incurred.

Often, the child is still very young in these cases, which must be taken into consideration when establishing the visitation schedule. At the same time, the child's age should not be the sole reason to limit a parent's time with a child. These considerations were discussed earlier in this chapter and are the same whether the parents were married or not.

Some complications arise from the lack of ties between the parties in some instances. For example, if the parties never lived together, the father has never had an opportunity to spend a great deal of time with his child. While this factor should not be used against a parent, it often is.

As for strategies to use, it is important to have the father begin paying child support voluntarily and if he can, exercise visitation as early as is practical. Every good faith effort on the father's part should be presented to the court to show his sincerity in wanting to parent and to support his child.

A complicated situation can arise where paternity has not been established, but the child's mother is not fit. Until the parentage can be established, the would-be father is not the legal father, such that he can be considered for custody. Therefore, as the practitioner, you must move as quickly as possible to establish paternity for the father.

Also in Alabama, we have the Alabama Putative Father Registry requirement. If the father fails to register, then implied consent can be inferred in an adoption situation. The father only has thirty days after the birth of the child to register. If you are representing an unmarried father, you must be aware of this potential pitfall that can have a dramatic effect in a case.

Domestic Abuse, Child Abuse, and Drug and Alcohol Abuse

Domestic Abuse

Every case with domestic violence allegations should be handled carefully and differently depending upon the abuse alleged. In these situations, if you are representing the abused spouse, you should interview that spouse thoroughly about each instance of abuse, including what was said, the circumstances of the abuse, and if the children were present. It is important to ask if the children witnessed the abuse, if they saw the aftermath, or if they heard the conflict. Some judges feel that even if there is domestic abuse, as long as the children were not present or aware, the visitation will not be affected. Other judges will restrict visitation until the abusive parent seeks counseling or anger management classes or only allow supervised visitation. As the practitioner, you must develop the facts of the abuse and the circumstances so that you can present a clear picture of the events that have transpired. The more detail you can discern, the better. If you can have your client write a narrative of what has happened, that is also useful for refreshing his or her recollection if the trial is months or even years later.

Child Abuse

Child abuse cases are the worst scenario for the children, the parents, and the families involved. It is important to get the children into counseling sooner rather than later. Even when being abused, the children still love the abusive parent and often want to be with that parent. It is important to involve counselors to help the children cope and to help the parents address the situation.

Be cooperative with investigators from the state child welfare agencies. If you represent the parent who reports the abuse, encourage your client to cooperate with the investigation and to act rationally. Otherwise, that parent may appear to have an agenda that is not in the best interest of the children. If you are representing the parent accused of abuse, be careful with whom they speak in the course of the investigation. If criminal charges may result, involve a criminal defense attorney to protect your client's interests and to make sure the situation is handled correctly. Criminal and civil proceedings can run parallel, and it is important to protect your client's interests in both proceedings. You may want to consider filing to stay the civil proceeding until the criminal proceeding has concluded. Remember, there is no such thing as the Fifth Amendment inferences in civil court. In fact, the court can infer that your client's refusal to answer the question means that the allegation is true. That is a horrible place to be.

Drug and Alcohol Abuse

In these types of cases, it is important to ask questions about whether the children were present while the drugs or alcohol was being abused. Was the parent abusing substances while caring for the child? How much alcohol is considered to be too much? Some clients may consider two beers to be too much, while others would not consider it to be abuse unless a case of beer was consumed. Where is the rational limit? Was the parent falling down drunk, but only on his noncustodial weekend, and when he has the children, is he sober? Do both parents drink alcohol? Is there drinking and driving with the children? Did the mother leave the child with the father knowing he was drunk? It is hard to argue at a custody trial the mother's disapproval of the father's drinking when she has voluntarily let the father care for the child while he was drinking and after he has been drinking.

With regard to drug abuse, does the parent have a prescription for the drug, but then abuses it? These are difficult cases because the court will give some people a pass if they have a prescription for the medication. It has to be demonstrated that the parent is abusing the prescription medication, has drug-seeking behaviors, takes too much medication and runs out early, and buys drugs to supplement the legitimate prescription. Did the parents both smoke pot together, but one parent got clean first? That can and does happen. In that situation you have to tread cautiously when hurling drug claims. If you are defending the parent accused of this abuse, you should recommend treatment, AA, or rehab to help show the court the parent's intent to control the problem. Then make sure the parent gets the treatment and is compliant. Sometimes the reason for the abuse is to mask another problem in the marriage. For example, a wife drinks to help cope with the emotional and verbal abuse by her husband. While it does not justify the alcohol abuse, it helps you as the lawyer handle it at trial. Unless the clients want to change, no amount of rehab, threats of losing custody, or any other penalties will get them to change their behaviors. These addictions are more powerful than even the threat of losing everything else, including their children.

False Abuse Allegations

On a related subject, there are cases where one parent makes allegations of abuse against the other parent to gain an advantage in a custody case. Personally, I find this reprehensible. As the accused parent, you are defending yourself against a negative—e.g., it did not happen and here is the proof. In this situation, you must pick apart the fabricated story. The credibility of the parties becomes even more important in this situation. Show other lies the parent has told, and demonstrate a motivation for the lies to help bolster your case.

Strategies for Successfully Litigating Child Custody Cases

The client is very important in a family law case. The client is the only one who has been living his or her life and is the only one who can tell you what happened. I try to get a complete list of all assets and debts, the history of the marriage, what led to the breakdown of the marriage, what the other side will say about my client, and what other potential problems we may encounter in the first interview. If something does not seem right about the story, I would rather ask sooner, than later.

The client needs to understand the process: discovery, temporary hearings, and trial. Some female clients think that just because they are the mothers they will win custody. You have to have a complete picture of who has done what to parent the children and what the other parent is going to say. For example, it is better to ask early who watched the children while your client was traveling for work. If dad was good enough to keep the children for that travel period, why can he not have joint custody now?

It is important to not make promises that you cannot keep or give your client false hopes or expectations as to what may occur. Some clients think just because they say something, that is the only version of the story the court will hear. Clients forget that their spouse also has a say.

I encourage clients to keep notes, journals, calendars of events, and significant happenings. They should make notes of significant things that happened during the marriage that relate to the children and the parents' roles with the children. Who was the softball coach? Who showed up for practices and games? If someone did not show up, then why? Who does the homework? Who takes the children to the doctor? How involved was each parent? All of these things must be developed in the first interview and as the case moves forward. I look at who can provide the most stability, consistency, and guidance to the children when considering who should get custody or how to approach a case. You cannot assume that person is going to be the mother, and you have to look at the totality of the case when evaluating your position. These cases are fact-driven and no two are exactly alike. If you know that you have a really bad skeleton in the closet, you need to look to settle the case for the best possible terms.

The attorney should consider the best arrangement for the client and the children. What facts, positive and negative, would impact the case if it were to try? Would you come out better at trial than with the offer? Can the client do what they are being asked to do? For example, can your client have custody of the children for thirty straight days in the summer, or would the client be better off with one week on, one week off, or even just long weekends and a couple of dedicated weeks for vacations? You have to try to tailor the agreement to what will work best in the real world, not just today, but tomorrow as well.

The old adage is that a successful settlement is one where everyone is unhappy. Both sides have to be willing to compromise on important issues to get to a settlement, but they also do not want to give away everything. A successful settlement is one where your client's needs are met and the children have the best possible outcome. As the lawyer, you have to help your client see the far-reaching ramifications and results of the settlement, not the immediate effect or appearance.

Alternative Dispute Resolution

Mediation can be very successful in divorce cases if both parties are willing to compromise and work toward a solution. Custody cases are hard to mediate as one side always feels it has lost if custody is lost. Children cannot be divided up like money. The clients are essential in the mediation process as they are the ones agreeing to a settlement that may not be what they considered in the first place.

I am reserving judgment on the collaborative movement for now. I can see good aspects of it, but if attorneys are committed to working toward a solution, rather than causing problems, then there should be no need for a collaborative movement. I do not see how it saves the client money, but proponents say it does.

Alternative Dispute Resolution (ADR) provides faster results than waiting on a trial date. ADR allows the client some control in the process rather than leaving everything up to the court. The backlog of cases has encouraged the use of alternative means to reaching an end result.

Cases where one party has to be in control and win are not good cases for ADR. Cases where both parents are committed to reaching a positive resolution for the children are good candidates for ADR. If the other attorney would rather the case be a boxing match than a search for a solution, the case will not resolve. Sometimes, clients need to hear from a mediator what is good and bad about their cases. It sounds different from a third party and that can help a case resolve.

Advice for Family Law Attorneys

It is important to remember your role as the attorney. If your clients need emotional support, encourage them to seek appropriate counseling. Often, attorneys are asked to fix things that are not fixable, or we are asked to make the spouse stop the very behaviors that are the reason for the divorce. You have to help keep it real. Do not let them fight over a TV once custody is settled. These cases are emotionally charged and draining, and as the lawyer, you have to try to take the emotion out of the situation as best you can.

It is important to explore the positives and negatives in the case. The client only wants to tell you the positives, not the negatives. Do not take everything at face value. Ask for proof and documents that support your client's contentions. Ask for medical records, counseling records, school records, cards, notes—anything that can support your case for custody over the other parent.

You need to prepare your client for the tough questions they will be asked in court and not sugarcoat how draining a trial is emotionally and financially. Psychological experts can help with parenting evaluations, and can help separate the truth from the fiction. They can help support the emotions of the client and channel those emotions. They can be a resource for the client to realize that their decisions are for the best interests of the child.

An expert can help the court decide what is best for the emotional health of the children. If you are looking to change custody, an expert can give justification as to why the current custodial situation does not work and what would work. They may not always be necessary, but they can provide additional testimony to the court to support your case.

It is critical to have a good relationship with court officers and judges. Your credibility can go a long way in helping your clients as their cases move forward. If the court knows you are trustworthy, it gives them confidence that you are not putting forward lies or wasting the court's time with a case. You must always exercise candor with the court and never let a client compromise your integrity.

Family law attorneys should be compassionate, knowledgeable, practical, rational, and able to articulate their client's desires in an effective manner. You have to be able to get along with others because you are not always going to have all of the facts on your side and will need someone else's help. Stay up to date on the law and the courts. You should participate in your state's family law section and listservs. Have a sense of humor and do not take yourself too seriously. Family law is not the "easy" area that other lawyers like to think it is. No other area requires you to know so many areas of the law and to deal with so many personalities and moving parts. You have to be able to multitask, yet stay focused on what you have to accomplish.

Approach cases rationally and thoughtfully. Do not fight battles you cannot win and that will hurt you in the long run. Do not take cases personally. Try to focus on what you can prove within the parameters of the law.

This area of the law has some of the best rewards and some of the worst heartaches. Be prepared for both. Have a good support system, good mentors, and older attorneys you trust to guide you as you develop as a lawyer. Lawyers that you can bounce ideas off are invaluable. It is always best to have someone willing to give you a second opinion or who can help you analyze your case. Listen to others and listen to what the other side in a case may be saying. Remember that there are two sides to every story in a child custody case, and somewhere in the middle is probably the truth.

Be respectful of other attorneys and the other side. The highest praise you will receive is a referral from an attorney you worked against who thought enough of you to send you a client.

Relevant Recent Case from Alabama

D.M.J. v. D.N.J.[1] When you have a true joint custody arrangement, the best interest standard is used for any modifications of custody. The court can look at the impact of the lack of stability by the mother such that the award of sole physical custody to the father was in the child's best interests.

K.T.D. v K.W.P.[2] The mother, who was the sole custodian, believed that she did not have to "co-parent" with the father. Sole custody does not allow a parent to use her authority to that right to the detriment of the child. The mother acted in an immature and unreasonable manner with the father and his family in addition to attempting to keep the child from spending time with the father. "[T]his court has recognized that a custodial parent's attempts to interfere with a noncustodial parent's relationship with the child should be considered in determining whether custody of the child should be modified." The trial court changed custody from the mother to the father as a result.

C.W.S. v. C.M.P.[3] It is error for the trial court to fail to provide a noncustodial parent with a "sufficient specified visitation schedule to rely upon, independent of the custodial parent's discretion."[4]

---

[1] *D.M.J. v. D.N.J.*, 106 So. 3d 393, 396 (Ala. Civ. App. 2012).
[2] *K.T.D. v. K.W.P.*, 2110531, 2012 WL 5458549 (Ala. Civ. App. Nov. 9, 2012).
[3] *C.W.S. v. C.M.P.*, 99 So. 3d 864, 869 (Ala. Civ. App. 2012).
[4] *See also, J.K. v. State DHR,* 103 So. 3d 807, 814-15 (Ala. Civ. App. 2012) (mother entitled to specific visitation schedule with dependent child placed in custody of maternal aunt); *Pratt v. Pratt,* 56 So. 3d 638, 644 (Ala. Civ. App. 2010) ("An order of visitation granting a custodian

Ala. Code (1975) Section 30-3-135:[5] Permits a trial court to award visitation to a parent who committed domestic violence or family abuse "only if the court finds that adequate provisions for the safety of the child and the parent who is a victim of domestic or family violence can be made." Thus, the award of supervised visitation was within the discretion of the trial court.

Martin v. Cowart.[6] Parties had a joint custody order by agreement. Later, the mother filed to modify the order because the father had only visited with the child on alternating weekends and they had never exercised true joint custody. The court reversed the trial court's finding that there had not been a legally sound reason to change joint custody and ordered the trial court to award the mother sole physical custody of the child and to determine a visitation schedule for the father.

Snoyman v. Snoyman,[7] Ala. Code (1975) Section 30-3-134,[8] states that in a custody modification proceeding "a finding that domestic or family violence has occurred since the last custody determination constitutes a finding of a change in circumstances." Further, Ala. Code (1975) Section 30-3-131 provides that in a custody case, a determination that domestic violence has occurred raises a rebuttable presumption that it is detrimental to the child and not in the best interest of the child to be placed in the sole custody, joint legal custody, or joint physical custody with the perpetrator of the family violence. The court should also take into account what, if any, impact the domestic violence had on the child. But the mother cannot just rely on the impact of the domestic violence to change custody; she must also meet the McLendon standard that "the child's best interests will be materially promoted by a change of custody, and that the benefits of the change will more than offset the inherently disruptive effect resulting from the change in custody." Further, the child's preference with whom to live is not enough to support a change in custody.

Johnson v. Johnson.[9] The case references that orders where siblings are separated are not favored. However, if there is a compelling reason for the

---

so much discretion over a visitation schedule that the visitation could be completely avoided if the custodian so desired should be deemed to be an award of no visitation and to be in violation of the rights of the noncustodial parent.")

[5] Ala. Code § 30-3-135 (West).

[6] *Martin v. Cowart*, 111 So. 3d 732 (Ala. Civ. App. 2012).

[7] *Snoyman v. Snoyman*, 108 So. 3d 514 (Ala. Civ. App. 2012).

[8] Ala. Code § 30-3-134 (West)

[9] *Johnson v. Johnson*, 66 So. 3d 784 (Ala. Civ. App. 2011.

separation, the judgment will be afforded a strong presumption of correctness. But in this case, the court found no reason to separate the children by awarding custody to each parent.

Conclusion

Child custody cases are the most difficult cases for a practitioner. Not only do you have the legal components, you have the emotions from the clients. It is important to keep abreast of the frequently changing rules in the case law and to talk with other attorneys about what they have seen. If you are going in front of a new judge, talk to others who have appeared in front of him or her. Find out their preferences. As best you can, try to control the situation rather than the situation controlling you. You have the chance to make a difficult situation better, but you have to be ready, willing, and able to do so.

Key Takeaways

- Joint custody has become a more common arrangement as in many cases both parents work.
- The client is very important in a family law case. The client is the only one who has been living his or her life and is the only one who can tell you what happened.
- A successful settlement is one where everyone is unhappy. Both sides have to be willing to compromise on important issues to get to a settlement.
- Alternative Dispute Resolution (ADR) provides faster results than waiting on a trial date. ADR allows the client some control in the process rather than leaving the impact up to the court.

Anne Lamkin Durward, a shareholder with Massey Stotser & Nichols PC, graduated from Cumberland School of Law at Samford University. She received her undergraduate degree in economics at Washington & Lee University in Lexington, Virginia. She is a fellow in the American Academy of Matrimonial Lawyers. Ms. Durward is listed in Best Lawyers in America and SuperLawyers in the area of family law. She is a frequent speaker in the areas of family law and probate law.

Making Effective Use of the Best Interest Test in Family Law Litigation

John F. Barnicle

Partner

Moncure & Barnicle

Introduction

The "best interest" test is the cornerstone upon which parental rights, residence, and contact judgments are based. While there are certainly elements in any case which are beyond counsel's control, adequate consideration of the best interest test does not need to be one of those elements. Early evaluation of the relevant factors may well enhance the prospects for success at trial.

The Emergence of the Best Interest Standard

Historically, American courts had a tendency to view parents unequally in the role of caretaker. The notion that mothers had a *de-facto* legal right to be the preferable parent eroded as the evolution of the workplace and society has shifted the traditional conceptions of parenting. Today neither parent is generally considered the preferable parent. Courts are now likely to show no preference for awarding custody (also referred to as "primary or shared residency" in some states) to either parent, but instead pursue a more objective analysis. While the parents, of course, remain a significant part of such an evaluation, each parent's gender has become increasingly irrelevant.

The modern day legal standard is more commonly known as the "best interest" test. In many states, that test is actually governed by statute, which enumerates nineteen criteria for the court to evaluate in determining the "best interest" of a minor child.[1] The best interest test codified existing case

---

[1] Me. Rev. Stat. Ann. tit. 19-A, § 1653(3) (2012), which reads:

> **Best interest of child.** The court, in making an award of parental rights and responsibilities with respect to a child, shall apply the standard of the best interest of the child. In making decisions regarding the child's residence and parent-child contact, the court shall consider as primary the safety and well-being of the child. In applying this standard, the court shall consider the following factors:
> A. The age of the child;
> B. The relationship of the child with the child's parents and any other persons who may significantly affect the child's welfare;
> C. The preference of the child, if old enough to express a meaningful preference;
> D. The duration and adequacy of the child's current living arrangements and the desirability of maintaining continuity;
> E. The stability of any proposed living arrangements for the child;
> F. The motivation of the parties involved and their capacities to give the child love, affection and guidance;
> G. The child's adjustment to the child's present home, school and community

law, which provided that, in making parental rights determinations, a court would generally "act as a wise, affectionate and careful parent."[2]

Among the advantages of the best interest test is that it provides an objective standard. As a matter of practice, counsel are well advised to

---

H. The capacity of each parent to allow and encourage frequent and continuing contact between the child and the other parent, including physical access;
I. The capacity of each parent to cooperate or to learn to cooperate in child care;
J. Methods for assisting parental cooperation and resolving disputes and each parent's willingness to use those methods;
K. The effect on the child if one parent has sole authority over the child's upbringing;
L. The existence of domestic abuse between the parents, in the past or currently, and how that abuse affects:
(1) The child emotionally;
(2) The safety of the child; and
(3) The other factors listed in this subsection, which must be considered in light of the presence of past or current domestic abuse;
M. The existence of any history of child abuse by a parent;
N. All other factors having a reasonable bearing on the physical and psychological well-being of the child;
O. A parent's prior willful misuse of the protection from abuse process in chapter 101 in order to gain tactical advantage in a proceeding involving the determination of parental rights and responsibilities of a minor child. Such willful misuse may only be considered if established by clear and convincing evidence, and if it is further found by clear and convincing evidence that in the particular circumstances of the parents and child, that willful misuse tends to show that the acting parent will in the future have a lessened ability and willingness to cooperate and work with the other parent in their shared responsibilities for the child. The court shall articulate findings of fact whenever relying upon this factor as part of its determination of a child's best interest. The voluntary dismissal of a protection from abuse petition may not, taken alone, be treated as evidence of the willful misuse of the protection from abuse process;
P. If the child is under one year of age, whether the child is being breast-fed;
Q. The existence of a parent's conviction for a sex offense or a sexually violent offense as those terms are defined in Title 34-A, section 11203;
R. If there is a person residing with a parent, whether that person:
(1) Has been convicted of a crime under Title 17-A, chapter 11 or 12 or a comparable crime in another jurisdiction;
(2) Has been adjudicated of a juvenile offense that, if the person had been an adult at the time of the offense, would have been a violation of Title 17-A, chapter 11 or 12; or
(3) Has been adjudicated in a proceeding, in which the person was a party, under Title 22, chapter 1071 as having committed a sexual offense; and
S. Whether allocation of some or all parental rights and responsibilities would best support the child's safety and well-being.

[2] *Jacobs v. Jacobs*, 507 A.2d 596 (Me. 1986).

provide the statute to their clients early on so that the client can understand the standard by which that aspect of the case will be judged. Practically speaking, counsel should discuss how the facts of the case, at least initially, match up against the best interest test. That may guide counsel and the client with respect to early resolution or may very well provide the client and counsel with what amounts to a task list going forward.

Modern practice has evolved alongside the change in standard. In turn, counsel should devote substantial attention to the best interest test and its application to a particular case. As the court has become obligated to incorporate the best interest test when determining a child's best interest, so too have the other parties often involved in proceedings—guardians, child protective workers, and even counselors are familiar with the standards when asked to make a recommendation to the court. Now, more than ever, it is imperative for counsel to make a conscious effort to incorporate the best interest standard into strategy, at an early stage.

How Domestic, Child, and Substance Abuse Issues Factor into the Best Interest Test

Issues and domestic abuse, child abuse, and substance abuse routinely arise in family law, and are, of course, highly relevant to the best interest test. Counsel handling cases that involve domestic or child abuse should understand, as much as possible, the science underlying the effect on victims of such abuse and understand that children are, in fact, changed by exposure to abuse and trauma.[3]

In working with a client accused of abuse, advising the client approximately so that they are willing and able to participate in counseling is important. For example, where the client has an anger management issue and can prove that he or she has taken steps to mitigate the problem, the client should have a better chance for success. Likewise, when a client has substance abuse issues, proactive enrollment in counseling or other programs may go a long way toward improving the image of your client before a judge (and even the other parent) at final hearing.

---

[3] *See generally* Bruce D. Perry, *Effects of Traumatic Events on Children: an Introduction* (Child Trauma Academy 2003).

In many cases, domestic abuse issues are addressed even before a divorce, separation or parental rights action is filed. When a case involves domestic abuse, it is likely there are also criminal and/or protection from abuse (i.e., restraining order) cases occurring simultaneously. This complicates the best interest determination, but it is still possible for a parent accused or convicted of domestic abuse to have contact with the children, under appropriate circumstances.

Protection or restraining actions may be filed by a party to gain a tactical advantage against the other. Restraining actions are often, unfortunately, granted before a party has a chance to discuss his or her options with counsel, and can substantially complicate a pending or future family matter. Courts consider such tactics a blatant abuse of the protection system, and have even incorporated this reprehensible conduct as a specific best interest factor for the court to weigh; however, in some states, a party must satisfy the "clear and convincing" evidence standard to prove the same.[4]

When a party seeks a protection order, depending on the circumstances, the court may allow for at least supervised contact in the interim period between hearing the protection matter and hearing the family matter. The court can also make arrangements for contact through individual third parties, third-party organizations or court-appointed supervisors. Even if the case does not require supervised contact, the court can also involve third parties to handle the transportation and transition between the children and the abusive spouse. This approach follows one of the core tenets of the best interest standard in keeping the child out of parental disputes.

In the case of child abuse, a parent or guardian may seek a protection order from the courts on behalf of the abused child. The court may provide temporary prohibitions or limitations to contact between the child and the abuser, depending on the severity or circumstances of the abuse alleged. Often, family cases involving child abuse occur simultaneously with criminal cases, and the criminal cases often contain a bail condition requiring the abusive party to avoid contact with the

[4] Me. Rev. Stat. ann. tit. 19-A §1653(3)(O).

children. The major difference in these cases, however, involves the state. In some states, for example, the Child Welfare Division of the state Department of Health and Human Services becomes involved automatically upon allegations of abuse. Upon an investigation supporting a finding of abuse, the Department initiates a child protective proceeding, which may also run in tandem with a divorce or parental rights action. Although domestic abuse in some cases does not dramatically affect a child's ability to have contact with both parents, a finding against a parent after a full child protective inquiry may of course have significant long-term consequences to that parent's rights of contact.

Substance abuse issues often require affected parents to face increased scrutiny from the courts. Among other consequences, substance abuse affects a parent's ability to earn an income; affects a parent's ability to make decisions; and far too often affects a parent's ability to create a safe environment to nurture a child. It is common for judgments to restrict use of alcohol and non-prescription drugs during, and prior to, contact with the child. Additionally, under appropriate circumstances, a judgment can incorporate testing requirements for alcohol or drugs.

Cases involving substance abuse often include simultaneous protection cases filed by a parent or guardian. Examples of this include circumstances when a parent is arrested for operating under the influence with the child in the vehicle, or when one parent exposes the child to other people (i.e., new partners) who abuse substances in the presence of the child. In these cases, courts will often entertain the protection order process.

It is important to counsel clients that courts evaluate the best interest of the children under the circumstances prevailing at any given time. This means that a parent who does not have contact the first year after a residence hearing (because of drug issues, for example), might well have a chance at gaining residence in a subsequent year if he or she has stopped abusing, and otherwise has acted in the best interest of the child. Rehabilitation is key and it is often the case that if the client can show a turnaround after the fact, the court can and will modify its order if that is in the best interest of the child.

The Rule of Guardians *Ad Litem*

Many states utilize guardians *ad litem* as officers of the court with a mission to perform an investigation and make a recommendation to the court in accordance with the best interest of the child standard. Guardians *ad litem* are appointed as the eyes and ears of the court to advocate on behalf of the children and recommend to the court what arrangement the guardian believes to be is in the child's best interest.

As guardians *ad litem* occupy a unique place in court, they also hold significant power. Guardians often have their own place in court, and are entitled to their own allocated trial time as well. A guardian is often able to access any information that is relevant to the best interest of children, including the children's and parents' medical and counseling records.

In addition to wielding significant influence, the guardian will often leave both parties unsatisfied. It is not uncommon for a guardian to issue a report more strongly in one parent's favor, leaving the other party unhappy.

It is important to find a guardian who starts from the premise that they will "do no harm." It can also be important to seek a guardian who does not routinely stake out an unchangeable position too early, as that can radically alter the case dynamics. Guardians can and should be willing to reconsider their recommendation through the end of trial, based upon all available evidence.

Retention of a guardian or parenting coordinator can be a difficult process. Because the cases are so fact-specific, and client-specific, it is virtually impossible to predict how a guardian or parenting coordinator will respond to any given case. Nevertheless, it is critical to conduct significant due diligence prior to retention of a guardian. Counsel's due diligence shall always include contact with others who have professional experience with the guardian or parenting coordinator.

Counsel should review carefully with the client how to work with the guardian and how important it is to provide the guardian with facts, as opposed to conclusions. The client should understand that they need to share the facts with the guardian and allow the guardian to make conclusions, and best interest recommendations, based upon those facts. It is generally much more helpful for the client to be the source of information, as opposed to counsel.

The Need for Cooperation, Communication, and Flexibility in Co-Parenting Arrangements

Historically, the primary parent shouldered much of the burden, helping the children with schoolwork and taking them to medical appointments during the week. The non-primary parent, on the other hand, was often left as the "play" parent.

Today, parents are more often willing to shoulder an equal burden in terms of daily caretaking. Although not all parents are suitable candidates for shared residence arrangements (or even for contributing substantially as co-parents), many parents have embraced the opportunity. Of course, the probability of a joint residency arrangement being successful depends, in part, on how willing the parents are to participate in good faith in such an agreement. Sharing of residency necessitates more cooperation than an arrangement in which one parent shoulders the majority of the time/responsibility.

Parents who equally share time with their children must also be able to communicate effectively. An equally shared residency is not always the best approach. For example, in determining whether an equal sharing arrangement is in the child's best interest, courts and parents must consider, as part of the best interest analysis, practical considerations such as how far apart the residences are and what type of work hours the parties keep.

Helping the Client Improve Their Chances of Gaining Residence

When arguing a residence case, the client should advocate for their child in an effective manner that includes hiring the right attorney and assembling support groups that help the client foster the child's best interest.

The client should think objectively about the child's best interest, and avoid taking inappropriate advice from friends or family members. This may be as important as retaining an experienced attorney who understands how the courts will apply the best interest standard.

During litigation, clients must temper how they react, because those reactions can leave lasting impressions with the guardian *ad litem*, the court, the other party, and ultimately the children. Counsel should advise their client of real-world examples (such as e-mail or text messages that were sent to the other parent without carefully considering the messages' ramifications, leaving the opposition with a stack of unhelpful messages and Facebook postings that may be severely damaging to the case).

One of the challenges of custody cases is that litigants often lose focus of the children's best interest. Family law clients are often at a difficult point in their lives, and it can be a challenge for the attorney to help the client weather the storm. Family law litigants are susceptible to a dynamic in which their attorney, or others, may tell them what they want to hear. It is, of course, critical that the client be able to hear the unabashed truth from their attorney. Without appropriate legal advice and emotional support, clients are likely to bring the acrimony and instability of the outside world into the courtroom.

Objectively Applying the Best Interest Test

When accepting a residence case the attorney must consider, at every step of the process, how the best interest test will come into play. For example, where parents live far apart and disagree about where their child will live, the parent who seeks residence in another state will improve their case by striving to involve the other parent (through online video conferencing, telephone calls, or e-mail, for example). A parent's ability and willingness to include the other parent is one of the factors in the best interest test.[5]

There are numerous sections of the best interest test that can be directly affected by the client and/or counsel's approach to the case. For example, one of the best interest factors is the duration and adequacy of the child's current living arrangements and the desirability of maintaining continuity.[6] Certainly, consideration of this factor would lead counsel to think carefully

[5] Me. Rev. Stat. Ann. tit. 19-A, § 1653(3)(H-J).
[6] *Id.* at § 1653(3)(D).

about their approach in filing or responding to motions pending the final judgment. In some circumstances, making concessions early on in a proceeding may unintentionally compromise a party's position.

Maine's best interest test has a "catch-all" factor, as do many states, in which the court must consider "all other factors having a reasonable bearing on the physical and psychological wellbeing of the child."[7] Because every case is different, the relevance of specific factors necessarily varies from case to case, and so application of the best interest test becomes a fact-specific and individualized process.[8]

Additionally, the relationship of the child with their parents is of course highly relevant, but also their relationship with any other persons who may significantly affect their welfare.[9] Here, activities as mundane as daycare arrangements can significantly affect the outcome depending upon who specifically is providing the daycare. Again, with knowledge of the best interest test, counsel is able to proactively consider the impact of various potential courses of action by the client.

Providing an Education on Co-Parenting and the Custody Process

Although parents may separate because they no longer get along, generally speaking, the first point the attorney should press with their client is the importance of communicating with the ex-partner. It is therefore important to counsel a client that demonstrating a willingness to go above and beyond what is required (to keep the other parent fully informed and involved) will improve the client's case.

Although communication with the other parent may be the last thing an emotionally wounded party wants, it is important for the attorney to reinforce that advice by recommending educational classes that teach co-parenting, especially as courts often require it.[10] Not only do these programs raise the profile of the client for court, but the subject matter

[7] *Id.* at § 1653(3) (N).
[8] *Cloutier v. Lear*, 691 A.2d 660 (Me. 1997).
[9] Me. Rev. Stat. Ann. tit. 19-A, § 1653(3)(B).
[10] For example, Maine's court partners with Kids First Centers, more information can be found on their website. Kids First Center, *kidsfirstcenter.org* (Last visited 9/10/2013).

discussed often has a meaningful impact on how a parent interacts with his or her children throughout a very challenging time. Additionally, joining an educational program for parents going through a divorce can help make the process less fearsome for a parent who has perhaps never encountered the legal system.

Clients can also be encouraged to conduct research online to learn about the court process and additionally find some answers to their questions about co-parenting. Likewise, there are numerous books available to help the client understand how to better co-parent.[11]

Effectively Using Mediation in Child Custody Cases

In many jurisdictions, the court will generally accept an agreement reached by the parties. For many, alternative dispute resolution (ADR) provides an effective venue for reaching agreement, even in some of the most acrimonious circumstances.

Numerous types of ADR are available in custody cases, and they are often effective. ADR can be provided through the court or a third party, and may sometimes take the form of an informal ADR directly with a guardian *ad litem*.

Mediation is often required in cases involving children. Often, the court sets mediation following completion of the guardian's report. While the guardian's recommendation is not binding, it sometimes (for better or worse) serves in practice as the decision's blueprint, and is thus a good tool to have on hand when working on a resolution. While it is not impossible for the guardian to recommend a final resolution satisfactory to both parties, it is more common for the parties to have varying views of the recommendation. Participating in mediation after the guardian has conducted an investigation is often more effective since the parties are aware at that point of the recommendation. If a qualified guardian files a report that makes sense, the parties often recognize its potential influence on the court's decision.

[11] ISOLINA RICCI, PH.D. MOM'S HOUSE, DAD'S HOUSE (Touchstone 1997) (1982). JULIE A. ROSS & JUDY CORCORAN JOINT CUSTODY WITH A JERK: RAISING A CHILD WITH AN UNCOOPERATIVE EX (St. Martin's Griffin 1996).

Mediation may also be more effective after the parties have had a chance to implement different parenting schedules. The court might order the parties to share their children on a week-to-week basis for three months, for example, to determine whether that schedule works. Mediation may be more valuable after such a trial run.

Although it is best to conduct the ADR after the guardian makes a report and the parties attempt different parenting schedules, the attorney still must consider how to posture the case as it moves forward. For example, the schedule that initially is in place will often affect the final contact schedule. In fact, one of the factors in the best interest test essentially examines the current schedule and how well it works.[12] This is why it is important for the attorney and client to understand the impact of the best interest test at the *beginning* of the case, and how those factors are relevant to the *rest* of the case.

Conclusion

Litigation concerning children is often not a clinical process with objective evidence (such as a breach of contract case, for example). Instead, most child custody cases involve more emotional, subjective issues and require the attorney to be able to communicate with people who can be emotional and upset. Bringing an angry client to court is counterproductive, but often getting the client to the point where he or she can talk objectively about the case can be difficult.

Family law attorneys have a unique ability to affect a client's outlook, since clients who have children at stake may not always think rationally. Among other things, it is important to provide the client with realistic expectations by helping them understand the best interest test, how the court is going to interpret that test, and what actions the client can take to be in the best possible posture at the end of the case.

This is a hands-on area of law, and the attorney and staff (including assistants and paralegals) must be willing to spend personal time with the clients, as well as answer seemingly endless telephone calls and e-mail messages in a timely manner. Clients in child custody cases are concerned about losing their children, and the attorney should always keep that in

[12] Me. Rev. Stat. Ann. tit. 19-A, § 1653(3)(D)-(E).

mind. It is also important to guide the client to the appropriate resources, including guardians *ad litem*, counselors, and parent coordinators. Before hiring such a third party, the attorney should conduct due diligence. In this manner, the attorney can help the client achieve the best possible results.

Counsel with in-depth knowledge of the best interest factors can best guide their clients so that their clients can take actions that are consistent with the best interest test.

Key Takeaways

- Consider how the best interest standard will affect a residence case when accepting it, and while counseling your client. Assist your client in taking actions that will help the client meet those standards. Review of the best interest test, and each specific factor, should be undertaken at the outset with a view toward improving your client's position by addressing any and all relevant factors.
- When determining whether an equal co-parenting arrangement is in the children's best interest, help your client consider practical factors such as how far apart the residences are and what type of work hours the parties keep.
- Help your client detach from the emotional part of the separation, and act in a way that demonstrates that awarding your client primary residence or custody is in the children's best interest. During litigation, your client must also temper their reactions to the process because those reactions can leave lasting and adverse impressions.

John F. Barnicle is a partner at the firm of Moncure & Barnicle in Topsham, Maine. His family law practice includes trials and appeals in divorce, parental rights, and related areas. Mr. Barnicle is a member of the Maine State and American Bar associations (Litigation Section) and the Maine Trial Lawyer's Association.

Mr. Barnicle received his BBA from University of Massachusetts and his JD from Syracuse University in 1982 and began practicing in Maine that same year. He has published legal articles and presented at continuing education seminars, and is a presenter in "Kids First" classes for parents involved in divorce or parental rights actions.

Appendices

APPENDIX A

CUSTODY TESTIMONY OUTLINE

We need letters from people who know you and the child(ren). We will turn these letters into affidavits that can be filed with the court. We would like the person writing the letter to first say how he or she knows you and your family and what interactions the person has had with you and your family, and then go on to consider the following things that my help them give us some insight into the situation. These letters, which are written to help you get custody, should address what the letter-writers know (if anything) about the following:

- Prior interaction between you and the child(ren);
- Prior interaction between the other parent and the child(ren);
- The relationships you and the child(ren) have with each other;
- The relationships the other parent and the child(ren) have with each other;
- The relationships between the child(ren) and other members of their extended family, such as aunts, uncles, grandparents, etc.;
- The relationships between the child(ren) and other children in the family;
- The relationships between the child(ren) and other children in your neighborhood;
- The relationships between the child(ren) and other persons in your neighborhood;
- The relationships between the child(ren) and other children in the other parent's neighborhood;
- The relationships between the child(ren) and other persons in the other parent's neighborhood;
- The amount of time you have available for the child(ren);
- The amount of time the other parent has available for the child(ren);
- The amount of time you actually spend with the child(ren);
- The amount of time the other parent actually spends with the child(ren);
- The child(ren)'s school schedule and either parent's involvement in the school and transportation to and from school;

- The child(ren)'s studies for school and either parent's involvement in helping with those studies;
- The need for or use of daycare for the child(ren);
- The involvement you have in the child(ren)'s medical care;
- The involvement the other parent has in the child(ren)'s medical care;
- Any special needs of the child(ren);
- The mental and physical health of each child;
- Your mental and physical health;
- The other parent's mental and physical health;
- Safety concerns for the child(ren);
- Health concerns for the child(ren);
- Each parent's willingness to cooperate on visitation;
- Whether either parent has been convicted of or pleaded guilty to any criminal offense involving any act that resulted in a child being an abused child or a neglected child or was the perpetrator of the abusive act or neglectful act that caused this;
- Any other relevant behavior or criminal record information;
- Whether you or the other parent is planning on moving (especially out of state);
- Your involvement in the provision of meals for the child(ren);
- The other parent's involvement in the provision of meals for the child(ren);
- Your involvement in the provision of medical care for the child(ren);
- The other parent's involvement in the provision of medical care for the child(ren);
- Your involvement in helping transport the child(ren);
- The other parent's involvement in helping transport the child(ren);
- Your involvement in home matters, such as cleaning and laundry;
- The other parent's involvement in home matters, such as cleaning and laundry;
- Your involvement in the provision of clothing for the child(ren);
- The other parent's involvement in the provision of clothing for the child(ren);
- Your schedule;
- The other parent's schedule;

- The child(ren)'s extracurricular activities and your involvement in them and ability to help with them;
- The child(ren)'s extracurricular activities and the other parent's involvement in them and ability to help with them;
- Discipline; and
- What is in child(ren)'s best interests regarding where they should be placed—who should have custody.

Courtesy of William L. Geary, Law Offices of William L. Geary Co. LPA

APPENDIX B

AFFIDAVIT LETTER COVERSHEET

IN THE COURT OF COMMON PLEAS OF xxxxxx COUNTY, xxxxxx
DIVISION OF DOMESTIC RELATIONS

Robert >>>>

CASE NUMBER:

JUDGE:

Plaintiff,

Magistrate

VS

Cynthia >>>>>>

Defendant.

State of xxxx)

County of ___________)

I, the undersigned, being first duly cautioned and sworn, state that I have personal knowledge of the facts stated in my attached letter, that those facts are true, and that any opinions expressed therein are my own opinions.

FURTHER, AFFIANT SAYETH NAUGHT.

____

Sworn to before me and subscribed in my presence this _____ day of the month of _____ 201__ .

____

NOTARY PUBLIC—State of xxxx

Courtesy of William L. Geary, Law Offices of William L. Geary Co. LPA

APPENDIX C

FIRST COLLABORATIVE MEETING AGENDA

First Collaborative Meeting Agenda

______________ and ______________

[Date of Session-TBA]

[Time of Session-TBA]

1. Introductory Issues
2. Review of Ground Rules and Collaborative Commitments.
3. Discuss payment of attorney fees.
4. Identification of Goals and Interests.

    a. ______________'s individual goals and interests.
    b. ______________'s individual goals and interests.
    c. Shared goals and interests.

5. Discussion of children's issues.
6. Discussion of living arrangements.
7. Identify other team members that may be necessary.
8. Identify immediate issues requiring resolution, if any.
9. Identify long-term issues requiring resolution.
10. Next steps/homework assignments.
11. Future meetings

    a. [List dates/times of future meetings]
    b. Agenda for next meetings.

Courtesy of Gloria Mitchell, Mitchell Law Group

APPENDIX D

COLLABORATIVE LAW PARTICIPATION AGREEMENT

Among: ______________, Participant—Husband
______________, Attorney for Husband
and
________________, Participant—Wife
________________, Attorney for Wife

1.0 GOALS

1.1 We, the Participants, believe that it is in our best interests and the best interests of our minor children to reach an agreement through the Collaborative process instead of going to Court.

1.2 We agree to use the Collaborative Law process to resolve differences. Collaborative Law is based on:

a. Honesty (full and complete disclosure of all assets, debts, and income);
b. Satisfying the interests of both parties;
c. Cooperation;
d. Integrity;
e. Professionalism;
f. Dignity;
g. Respect; and
h. Candor.

1.3 Collaborative Law focuses on our **future** well-being and the future well-being of our children.

1.4 Collaborative Law does **not** rely on Court-imposed solutions.

1.5 Our goals are:

- To resolve our differences in the best interests of our children;
- To eliminate the negative economic, social, and emotional consequences of litigation; and
- To find solutions that are acceptable to both of us.

2.0 WE WILL NOT GO TO COURT

2.1 *Out-of-Court.* We commit ourselves to settling this case without going to Court.

2.2 *Disclosure.* We agree to give full and complete disclosure of all information whether requested or not. Any request for disclosure of information will be made informally. We will provide this information promptly.

We acknowledge that by using the Collaborative process we are giving up certain investigative procedures and methods that would be available to us in the litigation process. We give up these measures with the specific understanding that we will make full and fair disclosure of all assets, income, debts, and other information necessary for a fair settlement. Participation in the Collaborative Law process, and the settlement reached, is based upon the assumption that we have acted in good faith and have provided complete and accurate information to the best of our ability. We may be required to sign a sworn statement containing a full and fair disclosure of our incomes, assets, and debts.

2.3 *Settlement Conferences.* We agree to engage in informal discussions and conferences to settle all issues. All communication during settlement meetings will focus on the property, financial, and parenting issues in the dissolution and the constructive resolution of those issues. We are free to discuss issues in the dissolution with each other outside of the settlement meetings if we both agree and are comfortable doing so. We are also free to insist that these discussions be reserved for the settlement meetings where both attorneys are present.

Each of us promises not to spring discussions on the other in unscheduled telephone calls or in surprise visits to the other's residence.

We understand and acknowledge that the costs for settlement meetings are substantial and require everyone's cooperation to make the best possible use of available resources. To achieve this goal, we agree not to engage in unnecessary discussions of past events.

2.4 *Communication.* We acknowledge that inappropriate communications regarding our dissolution can be harmful to our children. Communication with our children regarding the dissolution will occur only if it is appropriate and done by mutual agreement or with the advice of a child specialist. We specifically agree that our children will not be included in any discussion regarding the dissolution except as described in this Agreement.

3.0 CAUTIONS

We understand and acknowledge the following:

3.1 *Commitment.* There is no guarantee that we will successfully resolve our differences using the Collaborative Law process. Success is primarily dependent upon our commitment to the process. We also understand that this process cannot eliminate concerns about any disharmony, distrust, or irreconcilable differences that have lead to our marriage dissolution.

3.2 *Legal Issues.* The Collaborative Law process is designed to resolve the following legal issues:

- Parenting time;
- Financial support of our children, including unreimbursed medical and dental expenses of our minor children, and day-care costs, if any;
- Insurance (medical, dental, life);
- Spousal maintenance;
- Division of property and debts;
- Attorneys' fees and costs; and
- Other issues we may agree to address.

This process is not designed to address therapeutic or psychological issues. When these or other nonlegal issues arise, our attorneys may refer us to appropriate experts or consultants.

3.3 *Attorney Role.* Although we pledge to be respectful and to negotiate in an interest-based manner, we are each entitled to assert our respective interests, and our attorneys will help us do this in a productive manner. We understand that our attorneys have a professional duty to represent his or her own client diligently and is not the attorney for the other, even though our attorneys share a commitment to the Collaborative Law process.

4.0 ATTORNEYS' FEES AND COSTS

We agree that our attorneys are entitled to be paid for their services. We also agree that each of us will pay our own attorney unless otherwise agreed during the Collaborative Law process that one of us will contribute to the other's attorney fees or that marital assets will be used to pay both attorneys' fees.

5.0 PARTICIPATION WITH INTEGRITY

5.1 We will respect each other.
5.2 We will work to protect the privacy and dignity of everyone involved in the Collaborative Law process.
5.3 We will maintain a high standard of integrity and specifically shall not take advantage of any miscalculations or mistakes of others, but shall immediately identify and correct them.

6.0 EXPERTS

6.1 We agree to use neutral experts for any issue that requires expert advice and/or recommendation.
6.2 We will retain any expert jointly unless we agree otherwise in writing.
6.3 We will agree in advance as to the source of payment for the experts' retainers or other fees.
6.4 We agree to direct all experts to assist us in resolving our differences without litigation.
6.5 Unless otherwise agreed in writing, the neutral expert and any report, recommendation, or documents generated by, or any oral communication from, the neutral expert shall be shared with each of us and our respective attorneys and covered by the confidentiality clause of this Agreement.

7.0 CHILDREN'S ISSUES

7.1 We agree to act quickly to resolve differences related to our children.
7.2 We agree to promote a caring, loving, and involved relationship between our children and each parent.
7.3 We agree to work for the best interests of the family as a whole.
7.4 We agree not to involve our children in our differences.
7.5 We agree not to remove our minor children from the State of Indiana without the prior written consent of the other while the Collaborative Law process is pending.

8.0 WE WILL NEGOTIATE IN GOOD FAITH

8.1 We acknowledge that each attorney represents only one client in the Collaborative Law process.
8.2 We understand that this process will involve good faith negotiation, with complete and honest disclosure.
8.3 We will be expected to take a balanced approach to resolving all differences. Where our interests differ, we will each use our best efforts to create proposals that are acceptable to both of us.
8.4 None of us will use threats of litigation as a way of forcing settlement, although each of us may discuss the likely outcome of going to Court.

9.0 RIGHTS AND OBLIGATIONS PENDING SETTLEMENT

We will acknowledge the filing date of the *Verified Joint Petition for Dissolution of Marriage* for the purpose of commencing a dissolution of marriage proceeding.

We agree that:

(1) Neither party will dispose of any assets except (i) for the necessities of life or for the necessary generation of income or preservation of assets, (ii) by an agreement in writing, or (iii) to retain counsel to carry on or to contest this proceeding.
(2) Neither party may harass the other party.
(3) All currently available insurance coverage must be maintained without change in coverage or beneficiary designation.

10.0 ABUSE OF THE COLLABORATIVE LAW PROCESS

We understand that both attorneys must withdraw from this case if either attorney learns that either of us has taken unfair advantage of this process. Some examples are:

- Abusing our children;
- Planning or threatening to flee the jurisdiction of the Court with our children;
- Disposing of property without the consent of the other;
- Withholding or misrepresenting relevant information;
- Failing to disclose the existence or true nature of assets, income, or debts;
- Failing to participate collaboratively in this process; or
- Any action to undermine or take unfair advantage of the Collaborative Law process.

11.0 ENFORCEABILITY OF AGREEMENTS

11.1 *Temporary Agreements.* In the event either of us requires an additional temporary agreement for any purpose, the agreement will be put in writing and signed by us and our attorneys. Any written temporary agreement is considered to be made pursuant to a commenced dissolution proceeding and therefore can be submitted to the Court as a basis for an Order and be enforced, if necessary.

11.2 *Permanent Agreement.* Any final Settlement Agreement we sign shall be submitted to the Court as the basis for entry of a Decree of Dissolution.

11.3 *In Case of Withdrawal.* If either of us or either attorney withdraws from the Collaborative Law process, any written temporary agreement may be presented to the Court as a basis for an Order pursuant to the dissolution proceeding, which the Court may make retroactive to the date of the written agreement. Similarly, in the event of a withdrawal from the Collaborative Law process, any signed final agreement may be presented to the Court as a basis for entry of a Decree of Dissolution. To effect the Court's ability to issue an Order retroactive to the date of the written agreement, we will file a "Joint Notice of Proceeding Pursuant to Collaborative Law."

12.0 LEGAL PROCESS

12.1 *Pleadings.* Other than the *Stipulation and Order re: Collaborative Law* and the pleadings filed prior to the signing of this Participation Agreement, neither of us or our attorneys will permit any motion or document to be served or filed that would initiate court intervention during the Collaborative Law process pending final agreement.

12.2 *Stipulation.* After we reach a final agreement, one of the attorneys will prepare a Decree of Dissolution, Waiver of Final Hearing and Settlement Agreement for review and signature by our attorneys and us.

12.3 *No Court.* None of us will use the Court during the Collaborative Law process.

12.4 *Participant Withdrawal from Collaborative Law Process.* If one of us decides to withdraw from the process, s/he shall provide prompt written notice to his or her attorney, who in turn will promptly notify the other attorney in writing.

12.5 *Attorney Withdrawal.* If one of our attorneys decides to withdraw from the process, s/he will promptly notify their client and the other attorney in writing.

12.6 *Waiting Period.* Upon withdrawal from the process, there will be a thirty (30) day waiting period, absent an emergency, before the scheduling of any court hearing, to permit us to retain new counsel and to make an orderly transition.

12.7 *Previous Agreements.* All temporary agreements will remain in full force and effect during the thirty (30) day period.

12.8 *No Surprise.* The intent of this section is to avoid surprise and prejudice to the rights of the nonwithdrawing participant.

12.9 *Presentation to Court.* Accordingly, we agree that either of us may bring this provision to the attention of the Court in requesting the continuance of a hearing scheduled by the other or his/her attorney during the thirty (30) day waiting period.

13.0 DISQUALIFICATION

13.1 *Withdrawal of Attorney.* If either Collaborative Law attorney withdraws from the case, the other attorney must also withdraw unless a withdrawing attorney is replaced by another Collaborative Law attorney who agrees in writing to comply with this Participation Agreement.

13.2 *Disqualification in Subsequent Matters.* After termination of the Collaborative Law process, whether by settlement or termination before settlement, neither attorney shall represent his or her client in a subsequent non-Collaborative matter against the other party.

14.0 CONFIDENTIALITY

14.1 *Confidentiality.* All settlement proposals exchanged within the Collaborative Law process will be confidential and without prejudice. If subsequent litigation occurs, we agree:

a. That we will not introduce, as evidence in Court, information disclosed during the Collaborative Law process for the purpose of reaching a settlement, except documents otherwise compellable by law, including any sworn statements as to financial status made by us;
b. That we will not introduce, as evidence in Court, information disclosed during the Collaborative Law process with respect to the other's behavior or legal position during the process;
c. That we will not attempt to depose either attorney or neutral expert, or ask or subpoena either attorney or any neutral expert to testify in any court proceeding with regard to matters disclosed during the Collaborative Law process; and
d. That we will not require the production at any court proceeding of any notes, records, or documents in the attorney's possession or in the possession of any neutral expert. However, once discharged, the attorneys shall return the file to their respective clients, excluding attorney work product.

14.2 *Applicability.* We agree this Confidentiality provision applies to any subsequent litigation, arbitration, or any other method of alternative dispute resolution.

15.0 ACKNOWLEDGMENT

15.1 We and our attorneys acknowledge that we have read this Agreement, understand its terms and conditions, and agree to abide by them.

15.2 We understand that by agreeing to this alternative method of resolving our dissolution issues, we are giving up certain rights, including the right to formal discovery, formal court hearings, and other procedures provided by the adversarial legal system.

15.3 We have chosen the Collaborative Law process to reduce emotional and financial costs, and to generate a final agreement that addresses our concerns. We agree to work in good faith to achieve these goals.

15.0 PLEDGE

WE HEREBY PLEDGE TO COMPLY WITH AND TO PROMOTE THE SPIRIT AND WRITTEN WORD OF THIS PARTICIPATION AGREEMENT.

____

______________, Husband

Dated:____________________

____

______________________, Wife

Dated:____________________

____

____

Attorney for Husband

Dated:________________________

____

____

Attorney for Wife

Dated:____________________

Courtesy of Gloria Mitchell, Mitchell Law Group

APPENDIX E

COLLABORATIVE LAW MATERIALS

What is Collaborative Law and Practice?

Collaborative Practice is an emerging trend which allows divorcing parties to resolve disputes respectfully—also referred to as a "no court divorce"—while working with trained professionals, Attorneys, Financial Advisors, Coaches and Child Specialists.

The conceptual overview is varied among states and practices, but generally, each party enters into a contractual agreement, whereby they each agree to retain their own attorney, each of whom is specially trained in collaborative law. The parties, their attorneys, and any trained professionals appropriate to the case work together in a series of meetings to reach agreements without court intervention. If the process is not successful, the agreement provides that the attorneys will resign from the case and each party then retains a new attorney to represent them in court.

Perhaps the single most attractive concept financially in collaborative law is that the parties contract to work together respectfully, honestly, and in good faith to resolve issues and reach agreements beneficial to everyone involved, which requires a mutual up-front, honest disclosure of all relevant financial disclosure and documentation.

The concept can also involve adding on the team, recognizing that there are many needs to be met while parties are undergoing divorce, so in addition to trained attorneys, your team can include other collaborative law professionals to assist with emotional, financial, and child related and parenting issues. These include financial advisors, trained therapists, "life coaches" and other specialists, all with numerous networking and resources to help the process and to help the parties ease through this life transition.

The process can be defined by each individual, and can be a matter of individual contract; but generally, the concept envisions a series of meetings to address any issues, custody, financial and otherwise; and for each meeting, the appropriate coach or consultant acts as a neutral advisor, and the attorneys advocate, but remain civil and respectful.

If the process is successful, the agreement is drafted by the attorneys and becomes a settlement agreement and is filed with the Court with the appropriate Decree and Waiver of Final Hearing. Conceptually, as in mediation and all ADR processes, the hope is that parties are far more likely to abide by an agreement crafted by their hands, rather than an Order imposed upon them by a Court after a contested hearing.

What is Cooperative Law and Practice?

The terms are often used interchangeably; and arguably; we already all attempt to engage in being Co-operative with each other as we practice, particularly in the high conflict area of divorce, but this is a term of art. What's the difference between Collaborative Practice and Mediation?

In mediation, an impartial third party (the mediator) assists the negotiations of both parties and tries to help settle your case. However, the mediator cannot give either of you legal advice or be an advocate for either side. If there are lawyers for each of you, they may or may not be present at the mediation sessions, but if they are not present, then you can consult them between mediation sessions. When there's an agreement, the mediator prepares a draft of the settlement terms for review and editing by both you and your lawyers.

Collaborative Practice allows you both to have lawyers present during the negotiation process to keep settlement as the top priority. The lawyers, who have training similar to mediators, work with their clients and one another to assure a balanced process that's positive and productive. When there is agreement, a document is drafted by the lawyers, and reviewed and edited by you both until everyone is satisfied.

Both Collaborative Practice and mediation rely on voluntary, free exchange of information and commitment to resolutions respecting everyone's shared goals. If mediation doesn't result in a settlement, you may choose to use your counsel in litigation, if this is what you and your lawyer have agreed. In Collaborative Practice, the lawyers and parties sign an agreement aligning everyone's interests in resolution. It specifically states that the Collaborative attorneys and other professional team members are disqualified from participating in litigation if the Collaborative process ends without reaching an agreement. Your choice of mediation or Collaborative Practice should be made with professional advice.

What is the History of Collaborative Law and What are Other States Doing?

The term incorporates all of the models developed since IACP's Minnesota lawyer Stu Webb created Collaborative Law ideas in the 1980s.

In Collaborative Practice, core elements form your contractual commitments, which are to:

- Negotiate a mutually acceptable settlement without having courts decide issues.
- Maintain open communication and information sharing.
- Create shared solutions acknowledging the highest priorities of all.

What's the Difference Between Collaborative Practice and Conventional Divorce?

In a conventional divorce, parties rely upon the court system and judges to resolve their disputes. Unfortunately, in a conventional divorce you often come to view each other as adversaries, and your divorce may be a battleground. The resulting conflicts take an immense toll on emotions—especially the children's. Collaborative Practice is by definition a non-adversarial approach. Your lawyers pledge in writing not to go to court. They negotiate in good faith, and work together with you to achieve mutual settlement outside the courts. Collaborative Practice eases the emotional strains of a breakup, and protects the well-being of children.

The Goals of Civil Collaborative Practice

<u>A Pledge to Collaborate:</u>

- Solve problems mutually and privately
- Preserve key relationships
- Prevent draining, costly court battles

The important difference between Collaborative Practice and conventional litigation is the commitment to reach an agreement without going to court. The parties maintain control of the process and the decisions instead of relinquishing them to a judge or jury. To reach this goal, the parties agree not to seek court intervention by committing to stay in the negotiation process and focus on settlement by design from the outset.

Open Communication

Even in the best circumstances, a dispute can strain communication between parties; keeping the lines of communication open is essential for agreement. Civil Collaborative Practice provides for face-to-face meetings among parties with their respective lawyers, other advisors, and neutral experts as needed. Sessions are designed to produce honest, open exchanges and the expression of priorities and expectations through good faith negotiations.

When issues are discussed openly, problem solving is direct and solution-oriented.

Achieving a High Quality Agreement

Resolution is the Focus of Civil Collaborative Practice.

Collaborative process emphasizes identification of suitable solutions. Instead of airing grievances and polarizing parties, Civil Collaborative Practice creates a vehicle and an environment that helps parties reach a superior settlement by building on areas of mutual agreement.

Teamwork = Conflict Resolution

Conflict resolution involves considerations such as financial issues, public image, and future relationships, and managing dispute resolution is challenging and time consuming. One of Civil Collaborative Practice's attractive options is its team approach. You and your lawyer work together with other professionals, including financial consultants, coaches and other specialists as needed. Scheduling is on the parties' terms. Your team works together to streamline the process, control costs, and craft constructive solutions for your dispute's range of issues.

Focus on the Future

Disputes can be resolved without burning bridges or severing key relationships-especially important when long-term responsibilities and connections remain after the dispute is resolved. Civil Collaborative Practice preserves the health and continuity of important relationships by preserving respect, encouraging cooperation, and creating options and workable solutions.

To find Civil Collaborative Practice lawyers and other professionals in your area, go to the Find a Collaborative Professional section of this website and simply enter your zip code for a resource list.

Courtesy of Gloria Mitchell, Mitchell Law Group

APPENDIX F

COLLABORATIVE CONFIDENTIALITY AGREEMENT

Petitioner / Respondent, ______________, in person and by counsel, __________________, stipulates and agrees that he / she will be receiving through the collaborative process certain financial information from the Petitioner / Respondent, ____________________ during the course of this action concerning matters pertaining to his / her business ownership interests in ____________________; including, but not limited to, the following: businesses, business interests, corporations, corporate interests, assets, liabilities, business assets, business liabilities, corporate assets, corporate liabilities, investments, and any and all other property or business interests which are under Husband's / Wife's control, all of which information Husband / Wife claims is confidential. The intent of this confidentiality agreement is to protect against the disclosure of the private and confidential financial information which may affect not only Husband / Wife but also other individuals / partners with an interest in Husband's / Wife's business ventures.

To regulate the disclosure and use of such information while participating in a collaborative divorce process, and outside the scope of discovery pursuant to Trial Rule 26 of the Indiana Rules of Procedure,

IT IS HEREBY AGREED AS FOLLOWS:

All information which contains confidential information, including, but not limited to, information concerning the income, expenses, profits, and all other information that refers or relates in any way to the business financial affairs of any of the businesses will be deemed CONFIDENTIAL. Whenever possible, the information will be designated and / or marked "CONFIDENTIAL", but all information provided which relates in any way to the financial affairs of Husband / Wife, or his / her business operations, are agreed to be treated as "CONFIDENTIAL."

1. Information provided that is "CONFIDENTIAL" pursuant to paragraph 1, above, shall be subject to the following restrictions:

a. All persons acquiring such information, either directly or indirectly, by reason of discovery in this action shall use such information only for purposes of the collaborative divorce proceeding under this Cause No. ______________________, during the pendency of said collaborative process, and not for any other purpose. Should either party elect to terminate the collaborative process, then this agreement will be merged into pending litigation and filed with the Court;
b. Information relating to any of the business of personal financial transactions of Husband / Wife, or that is stated to by when provided, or otherwise designated and/or marked "CONFIDENTIAL" shall not be given, shown, made available to or communicated in any way to any person other than: (i) the Court and its personnel if necessary and (ii) the parties, their experts, counsel and advisors.
c. The termination of proceedings in this cause shall not relieve either party or any other person from any of the obligations of confidentiality imposed by this Order.
d. Whenever any "CONFIDENTIAL" information is introduced or used at a deposition, hearing, or other proceeding, such portions of the proceedings, which concern the "CONFIDENTIAL" information, shall be conducted under circumstances such that only those persons authorized hereunder to have access to such "CONFIDENTIAL" information shall be present.
e. If any agreed upon depositions in this action become necessary, of any non-parties, then Husband / Wife may designate as "CONFIDENTIAL" any testimony or other information disclosed in such deposition. Whenever any confidential matter or its contents is introduced or used at a deposition, or during this proceeding, such portions of the proceedings, which concern the confidential matter or its contents, shall be conducted under circumstances such that only those persons authorized hereunder to have access to such confidential matter shall be present.

2. All documents and other materials produced pursuant to this Order shall be maintained by counsel under seal at their respective

offices, or by the parties, at their private residences and in the office of any agreed upon experts, and no copy or reproduction of protected documents and other materials shall be taken outside these places at any time except pursuant to paragraphs 1(d) and 1(e) above.

3. This confidentiality agreement and protective order does not in any manner impair, restrict, or limit Husband's / Wife's ability to conduct any and all discovery allowed by the Indiana Rules of Trial Procedure, as modified by the parties' collaborative law agreement. Wife further acknowledges and agrees that the terms of this confidential agreement and protective order do not in any manner limit the right to full and fair disclosure by the other of all information material to this action.

Dated:______________ ________________________________

______________, Petitioner/Respondent

Dated:______________ ________________________________

____________________,CPA

Dated:______________ ________________________________

________________________, Attorney for Petitioner/Respondent

Prepared By:

(Attorney)
MITCHELL & ASSOCIATES
9959 Crosspoint Boulevard
Indianapolis, Indiana 46256
Telephone: (317) 815-5900
Facsimile: (317) 472-0966

Courtesy of Gloria Mitchell, Mitchell Law Group

APPENDIX G

VERIFIED JOINT PETITION FOR DISSOLUTION OF MARRIAGE

Co-Petitioners, _____________ and ________________, being first duly sworn, in support of this Petition, state as follows:

1. We reside at __________, and have resided in _________ County for a period in excess of three (3) months, and in the State of Indiana for period in excess of six (6) months prior to filing this Petition.
2. We were married on ____________.
3. There are ____ children born of our marriage, ___________, d/o/b __________, and ____________, d/o/b __________. Wife is not currently pregnant.
4. Our marriage has suffered an irretrievable breakdown and there is no hope of reconciliation.
5. **This cause shall be handled through the Collaborative Law Process. We are filing a separate Stipulation and Order Re Collaborative Law.**
6. We request that our marriage be dissolved and that the Court approve our agreement.

WE AFFIRM UNDER THE PENALTIES OF PERJURY that the foregoing statements are true and correct, dated this _______ day of _______________, 2013.

____
__________, Husband

____
_______________, Wife

Submitted by,

(Name of firm)

____

____

Attorney for Husband

(Name of Firm)

____

____

Attorney for Wife

Courtesy of Gloria Mitchell, Mitchell Law Group

APPENDIX H

ORDER APPOINTING LEVEL II PARENTING COORDINATOR

Petitioner/Respondent, ____________________________, having filed a Petition for Appointment of Parenting Coordinator, such Petition being a part of this Court's record. And the Court having reviewed the same and being duly advised in the premises now finds the same should be granted.

IT IS, THEREFORE, ORDERED THAT:

1. *Appointment.* The Court hereby appoints ____________ as Parenting Coordinator (hereinafter "PC") in this case, whose address and telephone number are: ____________________________________, and the parties shall immediately contact said PC for scheduling purposes.
2. *Expenses.* Petitioner shall pay ______% and Respondent shall pay _______% of the PC's fees, including any retainer amount, for joint services. In addition, the PC shall be reimbursed for any expenses incurred, including, but not limited to, photocopies, messenger service, long distance telephone charges, express and/or certified mail costs, parking, mileage, and other travel expenses. The PC shall have the discretion to report to the Court that the PC desires to charge either party separately for individual contacts with that party or joint contacts made necessary by that party's behavior. The Court shall have the power to review, reallocate and enforce the payment of the fees of the PC. In the event that the testimony and or written report of the PC is required for any hearing, settlement conference or court action by one or both parties, the PC's fees for such services shall be paid by both parties, in advance according to the estimate provided by the PC.
3. *Role of the PC (Determination of PC Level).* The Court orders that the appointed PC shall be (Check either or both Levels):

______ **LEVEL II.**

A. *Role of the PC.* The PC **shall** make recommendations and work to resolve conflicts between the parents involving the designated issues, which do not affect the Court's exclusive jurisdiction to determine fundamental issues of custody and parenting time. Such recommendations, negotiations, and education shall include strategies for enforcing any shared parenting plan and contact / parenting time schedule, for minimizing child–related conflicts between the parties, and for eliminating unproductive or harmful behavior patters by one or both parents.

B. *Authority of the PC.* The PC shall attempt to resolve conflicts between the Parties by recommendation, negotiation, education and discussion. Provided however, that the PC shall make binding recommendations if the Parties are unable to reach a decision through recommendation, negotiation, education or discussion. In such cases, the PC shall provide written documentation of the PC's binding recommendations to the Parties and their counsel at least two (2) days prior to filing such with the Court.

The recommendation is binding pending review by the Court. If there is no objection within seven (7) days of the recommendation being made, then the recommendation is binding pending a substantial change in circumstances such that the recommendation is no longer reasonable.

C. *Objection to Recommendations.* If either Party objects to the recommendations by filing a petition to the Court for a hearing, within the time limit, the Court shall hold a hearing on whether or not such recommendation shall remain binding. The hearing shall be an expedited hearing, and if possible shall be conducted by summary testimony from counsel. Counsel shall keep such objections and hearing specific and concise. No issues not raised in objection to the Recommendations shall be addressed by the court in this expedited hearing.

D. *Level of PC.* The PC shall file a recommendation with the Court when and if the PC believes it necessary to modify the Level at which the PC is operating.

4. *Issues for the PC to address:*

The PC shall always address the basic co-parenting issues which include but are not limited to the following list:

a. implementing any voluntary or court-ordered plan or schedule so that the child(ren) have continuous and consistent contact with both parents;
b. vacation and/or holiday schedules;
c. transportation issues;
d. methods of pick-up and delivery;
e. dates and times of pick-up and delivery;
f. childcare, daycare and babysitting issues;
g. extracurricular and enrichment activities;
h. bedtime issues;
i. diet issues;
j. clothing issues;
k. discipline issues;
l. healthcare management;
m. participation in parenting time by significant others, relatives, etc.;
n. in the case of infants and toddlers, increasing parenting time when developmentally appropriate pursuant to the Indiana Parenting Time Guidelines or existing court order;
o. educate parents on how to effectively;

    i. communicate and negotiate;
    ii. develop and apply parenting skills;
    iii. meet the developmental needs of their child(ren);
    iv. disengage from each other when engagement leads to conflict;
    v. keep their child(ren) out of the middle of their adult disagreements; and identify the sources of their conflict with one another and work jointly to minimize conflict and lessen its harmful effects on the child(ren);

p. monitor the safety issues on behalf of the child(ren);
q. monitor safety issues in those cases involving domestic violence;
r. monitor implementation of a voluntary or court-ordered parenting plan or contact/parenting time schedule and mediate the parents' disputes regarding such plan or schedule;

In addition, the PC shall address the following issues specific to these Parties (check all that apply):

___ recommend to the parents that one or both parents and / or the children avail themselves of available and appropriate community resources, including, but not limited to, physical examinations, random drug screens, parenting classes, custody evaluation, and individual psychotherapy; and if such a recommendation is made, the PC shall select and manage such treatment team, if the PC determines necessary;

___ write detailed guidelines or recommended rules to help the parents communicate with one another and practice implementing those guidelines or rules. If either parent lacks parenting skills, the PC shall work with that parent to teach the necessary skills or to refer the parent to an appropriate parenting skills course;

___ recommend a means of compliance with any parenting plan or parenting schedule in the Court's Order;

___ when the parents cannot agree on a resolution of conflicts, and when it is necessary to promote the child(ren)'s best interests, recommend modification of a parenting plan or contact/parenting time schedule, reduce such recommendations to writing, and provide them to the parents and to any attorney who represents either parent;

___ recommend a final decision on any parenting issue concerning which the parents reach an impasse, by submitting a written recommendation to the parties and their counsel, and the same shall be binding until further Order;

___ facilitate communication between the parents by serving, if necessary, as a conduit for information;

___ recommend, where appropriate, the institution or cessation of supervised visitation;

___ when the parents cannot agree on a resolution, make recommendations regarding religion, religious training and church attendance, when in the best interests of the child(ren);

___ recommend a final decision with regard to large changes in vacation and/or holiday time shares, when appropriate;

___ ____

____

5. *The PC shall not:*

   a. serve as a custody evaluator in the case;
   b. offer a binding recommendation for a change in the child(ren)'s primary physical residence, but MAY advise the parties or their counsel for the need of a review of custody or a custody evaluation;
   c. address significant financial matters between the parents;
   d. attempt to exercise judicial authority;
   e. be contacted by either parent outside normal working hours, unless the matter constitutes a genuine emergency;
   f. substantially alter the percentage of parenting time between parents.

6. *Meeting with the PC.*

   a. In fulfilling his or her responsibilities, the PC shall be entitled to communicate with the parents and their children, separately or together, in person or by telephone; with the health care providers and mental health providers for the parents and the child(ren); and with any other third parties reasonably deemed necessary by the PC. The parents shall cooperate with the PC and shall execute any releases which may be necessary to permit the above communication to occur.
   b. Each parent is responsible for contacting the PC to schedule and arrange initial appointments.
   c. The parents shall provide copies of all pleadings, orders and correspondence that relate to the issues to be brought to the PC. These documents shall initially be provided within ten (10) days of the date of this Order.
   d. Each parent shall direct any disagreement with the other parent regarding the children to the PC. The PC shall work with both parents to resolve the conflict, and, if necessary, will recommend an appropriate resolution to the parents and their legal counsel.
   e. The parents and all agencies shall participate in good faith in the dispute resolution process.

7. *Written and Oral Report and Court Appearances.*

   a. The PC may submit written reports to the parents and/or their counsel, if the parent is represented by counsel, describing any conflicts and the PC's recommended resolutions. The PC may also report to the parents and/or their counsel, if the parent is represented by counsel, with regard to parental compliance and attitudes regarding any element of the parenting plan or parenting time schedule.

b. A PC shall submit a written report to the parents and/or their counsel, if a parent is represented by counsel, at the completion of services, and may submit interim reports.
c. Copies of all reports shall be sent to the parents and/or their counsel, if a parent is represented by counsel, at least ten (10) days prior to any hearing in the matter.
d. When necessary, decisions of the PC shall be made orally and shall become binding when communicated to both parties orally. However, such decisions shall be communicated in writing as soon as practicable.

8. *Terms of Appointment.*

a. The PC is appointed for two (2) years, or unless discharged prior to the expiration of two (2) years.
b. The PC, at any time, may be discharged by the Court with or without petition from a party. The PC may be disqualified on any of the grounds applicable for the removal of a judge, mediator, or arbitrator.
c. The PC may withdraw from acting as PC in the case at any time and for any reason, provided that notice is given to the parties and their counsel.
d. At the completion of services, the PC shall forward a closing statement to the parents and/or their counsel, if a parent is represented by counsel. After the case is closed by Court Order, the PC may be available as needed to the family if reinstated by an Order of the Court.
e. *No therapist-patient relationship and/or privilege is created between the PC and the parents or the minor child(ren).*

9. *Confidentiality.*

There is <u>NO</u> privilege or right of confidentiality between the children, the Parties and the PC.

10. *Cooperation / Release of Information.*

The Parties are ordered to cooperate with the PC, provide all relevant documentation to the PC, and to sign any and all release of information forms, or otherwise provide all authority necessary for the PC to obtain all medical, educational, counseling, and treatment information of the Parties, the children or any other person as necessary to the role of the PC.

Further, the Parties, or their representatives are ordered to provide and gather all information necessary to the role of the PC, including but not limited to medical, educational, counseling and treatment information of the Parties, the children, or any other person necessary to the recommendations of the PC.

11. *Incorporation of Agreed Matters into Enforceable Court Orders.*

Although one of the goals of the PC is to encourage parents to harmoniously resolve shared parenting issues without the need for a Court hearing, the negotiated or agreed matters shall be memorialized in writing, signed by the parties, copied to counsel if the parties are represented, and submitted by the parties or their counsel to the Court for approval.

12. *Authority, Qualifications, and Expertise.*

This appointment is based upon the expertise of the PC as a qualified mental health and / or legal professional. Further the Court finds that such PC is entitled to judicial immunity pursuant to Indiana law.

13. *The Court Further Orders That:*

____

____

____

SO ORDERED this ______ day of ______________________, 200___.

____

JUDGE, ________ County Court No. _____

Distribution:

Attorney for Petitioner

Attorney for Respondent

Parenting Coordinator

Courtesy of Gloria Mitchell, Mitchell Law Group

APPENDIX I

PARALLEL PARENTING PLAN ORDER

The Court concludes the parties are high conflict parents, as defined in the Indiana Parenting Time Guidelines. The Court finds high conflict because of the following behavior(s):

___ a pattern of ongoing litigation;

___ chronic anger and distrust;

___ inability to communicate about the child;

___ inability to cooperate in the care of the child; or

___ other behaviors placing the child's well-being at risk: ____
____.

[OR The Court finds parallel parenting is appropriate to phase out supervised parenting time.]

Accordingly, the court deviates from the Indiana Parenting Time Guidelines, and now Orders the following Parallel Parenting Plan.

1. RESPONSIBILITIES AND DECISION-MAKING

   1.1 Each parent has a responsibility to provide for the physical and emotional needs of the child. Both parents are very important to the child and the child needs both parents to be active parents throughout their lives. Both parents must respect each parent's separate role with the child. Each parent must put the child's needs first in planning and making arrangements involving the child.
   1.2 When the child is scheduled to be with Father, then Father is the "on-duty" parent. When the child is scheduled to be with Mother, then Mother is the "on-duty" parent.

1.3 The on-duty parent shall make decisions about the day to day care and control of the child.

1.4 This decision making is not to be confused with legal custody decision making concerning education, health care and religious upbringing of the child. These more significant decisions continue to be the exclusive responsibility of the parent who has been designated as the sole custodial parent.

1.5 In making decisions about the day to day care and control of the child, neither parent shall schedule activities for the child during the time the other parent is on-duty without prior agreement of the on-duty parent.

1.6 Parents share a joint and equal responsibility for following parenting time orders. The child shares none of this responsibility and should not be permitted to shoulder the burden of this decision.

1.7 Unacceptable excuses for one parent denying parenting time to the other include the following:

a. The child unjustifiably hesitates or refuses to go.
b. The child has a minor illness.
c. The child has to go somewhere.
d. The child is not home.
e. The noncustodial parent is behind in support.
f. The custodial parent does not want the child to go.
g. The weather is bad.
h. The child has no clothes to wear.
i. The other parent failed to meet preconditions established by the custodial parent.

2. REGULAR PARENTING TIME

2.1 The parents shall follow this specific schedule so the child understands the schedule.

2.2 [ ] Mother, or [ ] Father has sole custody of the child. The noncustodial parent shall have regular contact with the child as listed below:

[ ] Every other weekend, from 6:00 p.m. on Friday until 6:00 p.m. on Sunday.

[ ] Every other Saturday, from _______ a.m. until __________ p.m.

[ ] Every other Saturday and Sunday from ______ a.m. until ________ p.m. each day.

[] ____

[] ____

3. SUMMER PARENTING TIME SCHEDULE (use only if summer is different than the Regular Parenting Time outlined above.)

3.1 Mother shall be on-duty and the child will be with Mother as follows:

____

____

3.2 Father shall be on duty and the child will be with Father as follows:

____

____

4. HOLIDAY SCHEDULE

4.1 Holiday Schedule Priority. The below detailed holiday schedule overrides the above Regular Parenting Time Schedule. For listed holidays other than Spring Break and Christmas Break, when a holiday falls on a weekend, the parent who is on-duty for that holiday will be on-duty for the entire weekend unless specifically stated otherwise. It is possible under some circumstances that the holiday schedule could result in the child spending three (3) weekends in a row with the same parent.

4.2 On New Year's Eve/Day, Martin Luther King Day, President's Day, Easter, Memorial Day, 4th of July, Labor Day, Halloween, Fall Break, birthdays of the child and parents, and all other holidays / special days not specifically listed below, the child shall remain with the parent they are normally scheduled to be with that day, as provided in the Regular Parenting Time Schedule.

4.3 Spring Break. The child shall spend Spring Break with Father in odd numbered years and with Mother in even numbered years. This period shall be from two hours after the child is released from school before Spring Break, and ending at 7:00 pm of the last day before school begins again.

4.4 Mother's Day and Father's Day. The child shall spend Mother's Day weekend with Mother, and Father's Day weekend with Father each year. These periods shall be from Friday at 6:00 p.m. until Sunday at 6:00 p.m.

4.5 Thanksgiving. The child shall spend the Thanksgiving holiday, from two hours after the child is released from school Wednesday until Sunday at 7 p.m. with Father in odd numbered years, and with Mother in even numbered years.

4.6 Christmas.

a. The child shall celebrate Christmas Eve, December 24, from 9:00 a.m. until 9:00 p.m. with Mother in odd numbered years, and with Father in even numbered years. The child shall celebrate Christmas Day, December 25, from 9:00 p.m. on December 24 until 6:00 p.m. on December 25 with Father in odd numbered years, and with Mother in even numbered years. At 6:00 p.m. on December 25, the Regular Parenting Time Schedule resumes.

Or

b. Other:____

5. TRANSPORTATION OF THE CHILD

5.1 The parents shall arrive on time to drop off and pick up the child. The parents shall deliver the child's clothing, school supplies and belongings at the same time they deliver the child. The parents shall always attempt to return the child's clothing in a clean condition.

5.2 When the child is scheduled to return to Father, then Father shall pick the child up at [ ] Mother's home or [ ] ____________________________.

5.3 When the child is scheduled to return to Mother, then Mother shall pick the child up at [ ] Father's home or [ ] ____________________________.

5.4 Special Provisions Regarding Exchange Participation: (if necessary)

Other than the parents, only _______________ shall be present when the child is exchanged.

____

____.

5.5 A parent may not enter the residence of the other, except by express invitation, regardless of whether a parent retains a property interest in the residence of the other. Accordingly, the child shall be picked up at the front entrance of the appropriate residence or other location unless the parents agree otherwise. The person delivering the child shall not leave until the child is safely inside.

6. EMERGENCY CHANGES IN THE REGULAR PARENTING TIME SCHEDULE

6.1 Although the child needs living arrangements that are predictable, if an unexpected or unavoidable emergency comes up, the parents shall give each other as much notice as possible.
6.2 If unable to agree on a requested change to the schedule, the Regular Parenting Time Schedule shall be followed. If an emergency results in the need for child care, the on-duty parent shall make the child care arrangements and pay for the cost of child care, unless otherwise agreed.
6.3 Unless the parents agree, any missed parenting time shall not later be made up.

7. COMMUNICATION

7.1 Communication Book. The parents shall always use a "communication book" to communicate with each other on the child's education, health care, and activities. The communication book should be a spiral or hardbound notebook. The communication book will travel with the child, so that information about the child will be transmitted between the parents with minimal contact between parents.
7.2 Neutrality of the Child. To keep the child out of the middle of the parents' relationship and any conflict that may arise between the parents, the parents shall not:

7.1.1 Ask the child about the other parent, or
7.1.2 Ask the child to give messages to the other parent, or
7.1.3 Make unkind or negative statements about the other parent around the child.
7.1.4 Allow other people to make unkind or negative statements about the other parent around the child.

7.3 Dignity and Respect. The parents shall treat each other with dignity and respect in the presence of the child. The parents shall keep conversations short and calm when exchanging the child so the child will not become afraid or anxious.

7.4 Telephone Contact. The child may have private telephone access to the other parent [ ] at all times or [ ] between the hours of _______ and _______. The parents shall encourage and help the child stay in touch with the other parent.

7.5 The parents shall not interfere with communication between the child and the other parent by actions such as: refusing to answer a phone or refusing to allow the child or others to answer; recording phone conversations between the other parent and the child; turning off the phone or using a call blocking mechanism or otherwise denying the other parent telephone contact with the child.

7.7 Notice of Travel. Before leaving on out of town travel, the parents shall provide each other the address and phone number where the child can be reached if they will be away from home for more than 48 hours.

7.8 The parents shall at all times keep each other advised of their home and work addresses and telephone numbers. Notice of any change in this information shall be given to the other parent in the communication book at the next exchange.

8. SAFETY (use the following provisions only as necessary)

8.1 Neither parent shall operate a vehicle when impaired by use of alcohol or drugs.

8.2 [] Mother []Father [] Both parents shall not use alcohol or non-prescribed drugs when they are the on-duty parent.

8.3 The parents shall not leave the child _________ unattended at any time.

8.4 [] Mother []Father [] Both parents shall not use, nor allow anyone else to use, physical discipline with the child.

8.5 ________________ shall not use physical discipline with the child.

8.6 All contact between the child and ________________ shall be supervised by ____________________.

8.7 Neither parent shall allow the child to be in the presence of ____

9. EDUCATION

9.1 The custodial parent shall determine where the child attends school.
9.2 Both parents shall instruct the child's schools to list each parent and their respective addresses and telephone numbers on the school's records.
9.3 Each parent will maintain contact with the child's schools to find out about the child's needs, progress, grades, parent-teacher conferences, and other special events.
9.4 The parents shall use the "communication book" to share information about the child's school progress, behavior and events.

10. EXTENDED FAMILY

10.1 The child will usually benefit from maintaining ties with grandparents, relatives and people important to them. The parents shall help the child continue to be in contact with these people.
10.2 However, as provided above at "SAFETY,"

[ ] all contact between the child and ________________ shall be supervised by ____________________

[ ] neither parent shall allow the child to be in the presence of ____

11. CHILD CARE

11.1 Arranging for normal, day-to-day work-related child care for the child is the responsibility of the [ ] custodial parent [ ] on-duty parent.
11.2 When occasional other situations require child care for the child when the child is with the on-duty parent, the on-duty parent is not required to offer the other parent the chance to provide this care before seeking someone else to care for the child. However, in such situations, the on-duty parent shall make any needed occasional child care arrangements, and the on-duty parent shall pay the cost of that child care.
11.3 Only the following listed persons may provide occasional child care for the child: ____________________________________.
11.4 If the [ ] Mother [ ] Father anticipates being unable to personally supervise the child during the parent's entire schedule on-duty

time, the [ ] Mother [ ] Father must notify the other parent as soon as possible, and that parent's on-duty time for that [] day [] weekend will be cancelled, and not made up at any later time.

12. HEALTH CARE

12.1 Major decisions about health care (such as the need for surgery, glasses, contacts, prescription medications, orthodontia, etc., and the need for regular, on-going medical appointments and treatments, etc.) shall be made by the custodial parent.

12.2 Each parent has a right to the child's medical, dental, optical and other health care information and records. Each parent will contact the child's heath care providers to find out about the child's heath care needs, treatments and progress. The custodial parent shall give written authorization to the child's health care providers, permitting an ongoing release of all information regarding the child to the non-custodial parent including the right of the provider to discuss the child's situation with the non-custodial parent.

12.3 The parents shall use the "communication book" to communicate with each other on all health care issues for the child.

12.4 The on-duty parent shall make sure the child takes all prescription medication and follow all prescribed health care treatments.

12.5 In medical emergencies concerning the child, the on-duty parent shall notify the other parent of the emergency as soon as it is possible. In such emergencies, each parent can consent to emergency medical treatment for the child, as needed.

13. RELOCATION FROM CURRENT RESIDENCE

13.1 When either parent considers a change of residence, a 90 day advance notice of the intent to move must be provided to the other parent and filed with the court.

13.2 The Indiana Parenting Time Guidelines have a more detailed discussion of the statutory notice requirements at Section I.E.4, "Relocation."

14. EVENT ATTENDANCE

14.1 When the child is attending their sports team, club, religious, or other such events at school or elsewhere, [ ] only the on-duty parent [ ] both parents may attend the event.

14.2 The custodial parent is permitted to enroll the child in ________________ extracurricular activity. The non-custodial parent shall encourage this participation.

15. A CHILD'S BASIC NEEDS

To insure more responsible parenting and to promote the healthy adjustment and growth of the child, each parent should recognize and address the child's basic needs. Those needs include the following:

15.1 To know that the parents' decision to live apart is not the child's fault.
15.2 To develop and maintain an independent relationship with each parent and to have the continuing care and guidance from each parent.
15.3 To be free from having to side with either parent and to be free from conflict between the parents.
15.4 To have a relaxed, secure relationship with each parent without being placed in a position to manipulate one parent against the other.
15.5. To enjoy consistent time with each parent.
15.6. To be financially supported by each parent, regardless of how much time each parent spends with the child.
15.7. To be physically safe and adequately supervised when in the care of each parent and to have a stable, consistent and responsible child care arrangement when not supervised by a parent.
15.8. To develop and maintain meaningful relationships with other significant adults (grandparents, stepparents and other relatives) as long as these relationships do not interfere with or replace the child's primary relationship with the parents.

16. RESOLVING DISPUTES

16.1 Because this is an Order of the court, both parents must continue to follow this Parallel Parenting Plan even if the other parent does not.
16.2 When the parents cannot agree on the meaning or application of some part of this Parallel Parenting Plan, or if a significant change (such as a move or remarriage) causes conflict between the parents, both parents shall make a good faith effort to resolve those differences before returning to the court for relief. In most

situations, the court will require the parents to attend mediation before any court hearing will be conducted.

16.3 The parties shall attend ________________________ counseling / parenting education program.

DATE: ______, 201__ ____________________________________

COMMISSIONER/MAGISTRATE/JUDGE

The above entry is adopted as the Order of the Court on this same date.

____

JUDGE

Copies to: Attorney for Petitioner,

Attorney for Respondent,

Mediator:

DATE OF NOTICE:

INITIAL OF PERSON WHO NOTIFIED PARTIES: COURT CLERK OTHER

Courtesy of Gloria Mitchell, Mitchell Law Group

APPENDIX J

AGREED ENTRY AS TO PARENTING TIME

Petitioner, ________, in person and by counsel, _________, and Respondent, __________, in person and by counsel, __________, and for their Agreed Entry, agree and state as follows:

1. The parties agree to adopt and abide by the Indiana Parenting Time Guidelines, with the following exceptions:

   a. On those weekends during which Father exercises his weekend parenting time, said parenting time shall begin when the child's school is dismissed on Friday afternoon and shall extend until Monday morning, at which point Father shall take the child to school and Father's weekend parenting time shall end. If the child does not have school that day, due to school not being in session, Father's parenting time shall continue until 7:30 p.m. on Monday. If on the Friday on which Father's parenting time begins the child does not have school due to school not being in session, Father's parenting time shall begin Friday morning at 9:00 a.m.
   b. Father's mid-week parenting time shall begin at the time the child's school is dismissed on Wednesday afternoon, and shall last until Thursday morning, at which time Father shall be responsible for bringing the child to school. On those occasions when school is not in session, it will be Mother's responsibility to retrieve the child at the conclusion of Father's mid-week parenting time, at 9:00 a.m. Thursday morning.
   c. On the Mondays following Mother's regularly scheduled parenting time weekends, Father is to have parenting time with the child beginning when the child's school is dismissed on Monday afternoon and ending at 7:30 p.m. This parenting time shall not occur if the Monday in question is a school holiday whereby school is not in session, in which case Mother's weekend parenting time shall include Monday and there will be no parenting time make up for Father.
   d. In the event Father will be unwilling or unable to drive the child to school Monday morning following a parenting time

weekend with Father, Father shall give Mother 48 hours' notice and Mother will pick up the child at 7:30 p.m. Sunday evening. In the event Father will be unwilling or unable to drive the child to school Thursday morning following a mid-week parenting time session with Father, Father shall give Mother 48 hours' notice and Mother will pick up the child at 7:30 p.m. Wednesday evening.

e. When Father has parenting time on school nights, Father is to have the child's homework completed by the time the child is picked up by Mother. On those evenings when Father's parenting time ends at 7:30 p.m., Father is to have fed the child dinner prior to Mother picking the child up.

f. If the child is late to school more than three (3) times in one semester (which equals two (2) quarters) because Father did not get the child to school on time, then Father's overnight parenting time on school nights shall end, and until further Order of the Court or Agreement of the parties, Father's parenting time shall last until 7:30 p.m. on the respective school nights. The parties agree that if Father brings the child to school late due to circumstances which Father reasonably could not have prevented or avoided, said tardy will not count towards Father's total for the semester. Regardless of the reason for the tardy, Father shall advise Mother within 24 hours anytime the child has been late to school during Father's parenting time.

g. The parties agree that the clothing requirement described in the Indiana Parenting Time Guidelines, Section I(B)(3) shall not apply in their case.

h. *Fall Break.* The parties shall alternate having parenting time with the child during Fall Break for as long as the child has a scheduled Fall Break, with Mother having parenting time in odd years and Father having parenting time in even years. The Fall Break holiday is to begin at the dismissal of school and conclude at the beginning of the first school day following the Fall Break such that any regularly scheduled Wednesday evening parenting time for Father is not subject to make up.

c. *Extended Summer Parenting Time.* By April 1st of each year, Father is to notify Mother as to whether or not he is taking his one-half of the summer in one block of five consecutive weeks or if he is going to divide it into two segments of one three-week segment and one two-week segment. If Father chooses to exercise extended parenting time in two segments, then Father shall pick his three-week period after which Mother shall pick her three-week period, after which Father shall select his two-week period, which will then leave Mother with a two-week period. Father's selection shall not prohibit Mother from exercising two consecutive weeks of parenting time in the summer. The parties may agree to deviate from the Parenting Time Guidelines requiring that summer parenting time be exercised in consecutive weeks; however, the total number of weeks of extended summer parenting time shall not exceed one-half of the summer for either parent.

j. *Thanksgiving.* During those years when the child's birthday falls during the Thanksgiving holiday weekend, the Thanksgiving holiday parenting time right shall take precedence over the parenting time right associated with the child's birthday. Thanksgiving holiday shall commence at the dismissal of school on the last school day prior to Thanksgiving break, and conclude at the beginning of the first school day following the Thanksgiving holiday. Any regularly scheduled parenting time for Father on Wednesday of Thanksgiving break is not subject to make up.

2. The parties agree that no one under the age of fifteen (15) years will babysit the child absent agreement of both parties
3. Both parties will make their best efforts to be available to the other party to assist in caring for the child, including, but not limited to, those times when the child is ill.
4. The parties agree to no longer use the child's book bag to communicate with each other.
5. The parties agree that home e-mail accounts shall be the primary method of communication between them, although both parties recognize some situations may make e-mail communication impractical or detrimental to the child's best interests. Both parties agree that their first choice of communication will be home e-mail.
6. The parties agree to attend at least eight (8) counseling sessions in the twelve (12) months following the date of this Agreed Entry, at

a rate of no less than one (1) session per month. The parties agree to divide the costs of said counseling sessions equally. In the event either party fails to pay his or her half of the cost in a timely manner, the other party is released from the requirement to attend the counseling sessions. If the parties both agree, the parties may attend more than eight (8) sessions, however the parties must continue to divide the cost equally.

7. On the one-year anniversary of the date of this Agreed Entry, the parties agree to attend four (4) counseling sessions in the twelve (12) months following said anniversary date at a rate of no less than one session per month. The parties agree to divide the costs of said counseling sessions equally. In the event either party fails to pay their half of the cost in a timely manner, the other party is released from the requirement to attend the counseling sessions. This requirement shall be renewed every year on the anniversary date of this Agreement. If the parties both agree, the parties may attend more than four sessions, however the parties must continue to divide the cost equally.
8. The issue of whether either party shall pay any portion of the other party's attorney fees shall be reserved for hearing, to be heard at the Court's discretion; the parties agree that at said hearing, either party may present evidence in addition to "ability to pay" evidence, including, but not limited to, custody evaluations and exhibits related to said custody evaluations may be introduced and discussed in testimony.
9. All terms from previous Orders not modified herein shall remain in full force and effect.

WHEREFORE, the parties request the Court approve their Agreed Entry on the terms and conditions herein.

We affirm the foregoing represents the terms and conditions of our agreement and affix our signatures hereto.

_______________________	_______________________
Petitioner	Respondent
_______________________	_______________________
Attorney for Petitioner	Attorney for Respondent

ORDER

COMES NOW the Court and being duly advised in the premises finds the attached Agreed Entry should be, and hereby is, granted in all respects.

SO ORDERED this ___ day of ___________, 200___.

____
JUDGE

Courtesy of Gloria Mitchell, Mitchell Law Group

APPENDIX K

STIPULATION AND ORDER RE COLLABORATIVE LAW

The parties each stipulate as set forth below, and further stipulate that Orders shall be entered as follows which shall remain in effect until and unless modified by written agreement signed by both parties or further Court Order, whichever first occurs. This Stipulation is intended to be a binding Court Order upon being signed by the parties and the Court.

Attorney Representation

Attorney _______________ has been retained by Co-Petitioner, _______________, to advise him / her during the course of this proceeding, and Attorney _________________ has been retained by Co-Petitioner, _________________, to advise him / her during the course of this proceeding. The parties acknowledge that there is no privity of contract by virtue of the execution of this Stipulation and Order. Each attorney represents only his or her client; neither attorney represents his or her client's spouse. While the respective attorneys are parties to this agreement and are committed to negotiation in an atmosphere of honesty and integrity, the parties understand and agree they cannot rely upon the attorney representing their spouse to provide representation, legal advice or information. Furthermore, the parties understand and agree that the attorneys, by virtue of this agreement, do not have an affirmative obligation to disclose confidential information the client requests remain confidential. Each party shall rely exclusively upon the legal advice and representation provided to them by his or her own counsel and shall have no right to claim that he or she received legal advice or representation from the other party's counsel. Each attorney agrees to be fully bound by the terms and provisions of this Stipulation and Order. Each attorney is disqualified from appearing as attorney of record for either party in any contested matter in this proceeding or in any other contested family law matter involving both parties. This disqualification shall survive the terms of this Stipulation and Order.

Notwithstanding the above, the attorneys named above may appear as counsel of record for purposes of filing all documents reflecting the agreement of the parties in reaching a resolution of their Collaborative Law dissolution and attending the final hearing.

Collaborative Law Process

Both parties and attorneys agree to treat this matter as a Collaborative Law dissolution. For so long as this Stipulation and Order is in effect, the parties and attorneys agree to devote all of their efforts to obtain a negotiated settlement in an efficient, cooperative manner pursuant to the terms of this stipulation and agree that neither party nor attorney named in this Stipulation will file any document requesting intervention by the Court unless mutually agreed on by all concerned.

Additional Restraining Orders

Both parties agree that, immediately:

1. Each is restrained from borrowing against, canceling, transferring, disposing of, or changing the beneficiaries of any insurance or any other coverage including life, health, automobile and/or disability held for the benefit of the parties or their minor children.
2. Each party shall notify the other of any proposed extraordinary expenditures at least five (5) business days prior to incurring these extraordinary expenditures and account to the other party for all extraordinary expenditures made after these restraining orders are effective; and
3. Except for uninsured healthcare expenses for the parties' children, neither party shall incur any debts or liabilities for which the other may be held responsible.

The foregoing orders may be modified by mutual agreement.

Expert Witnesses

The parties agree that any experts retained or employed in the Collaborative Law process shall be retained by both parties.

Except upon the mutual written agreement of the parties to the contrary, any person or firm retained by either party or attorney, or whose work product is used by either party or attorney, during the term of this Stipulation and Order, is disqualified from appearing as an expert witness for either party to testify as to any matter related to such person's or firm's work product in the Collaborative Law process. Unless the parties agree otherwise, all notes, work papers, summaries and reports shall be inadmissible as evidence in any proceeding involving these parties, but shall be furnished to successor counsel and shall be available for non-evidentiary use in litigated proceedings. Such persons or firms include, but are not limited to, accountants, attorneys, mental health professionals, personal or real property valuation experts, vocational consultants, private investigators, doctors or any persons retained or employed in the Collaborative Law process.

Disclosure and Discovery

Both parties shall provide each other with any written authorizations requested which may be required in order to obtain information or documentation, or to prepare Qualified Domestic Relations Orders or other orders facilitating agreements reached. The parties and attorneys acknowledge and understand that honesty and the full disclosure of all relevant financial information is an integral factor in the success of a Collaborative Law case.

All discovery requests shall be made informally. No Motion to Compel or Motion for Sanctions is available for any discovery requests made during the term of this Stipulation and Order. Responses to any discovery requests made during the term of this Stipulation and Order should be made within the time limits prescribed by applicable statute or Local Rule. All responses to discovery requests shall be verified by the party responding and subject to penalty if false.

Attorney Fees

The Court may award attorney fees and impose sanctions in the event that any party or attorney has (i) used the Collaborative Law process in bad faith for the purpose of unilateral delay, or (ii) engaged in any concealment, misrepresentation, or perpetuation of the same in any way that materially and adversely affects the rights of the other party.

Statements of Parties and Attorneys

All settlement documents shall be inadmissible for any purpose in any subsequent proceeding except as otherwise agreed upon between the parties. Statements made by either party during the four-way meetings shall be protected as if the statements were made in mediation, and no such communications shall be deemed a waiver of any privilege by any party. However, statements that indicate an intent or disposition to do any of the following actions are not privileged; to endanger the health or safety of the other party, or of the children; to conceal or change the residence of the children; to commit irreparable economic damage to the property of either party; or to conceal income or assets.

Termination of Collaborative Status

Either party or attorney may withdraw from this matter unilaterally by giving thirty (30) days' written notice of such election to the other party and attorney. Notice of Withdrawal does not terminate the Collaborative Law process; a party losing his or her attorney may continue in the Collaborative Law Process with a new attorney who will agree in writing to be bound by this Stipulation and Order and the above-referenced Guidelines and Principles.

Upon termination of the process or withdrawal of any counsel, such affected attorney will promptly cooperate to facilitate the transfer of the client's matter to successor counsel.

The parties do not waive their right to seek the assistance of the Court; however, any resort to litigation results in the automatic termination of the Collaborative Law Process and the disqualification of the undersigned attorneys, effective the date any application to the Court for its orders or otherwise made. In the event of the termination of the collaborative process, this matter will continue to remain in the Court as a non-collaborative case.

Verification

I affirm under the penalties for perjury that the representations contained in the foregoing *Stipulation and Order* are true, all to the best of my knowledge and belief.

______________________________	______________________________
________________, Husband	________________, Wife
Dated:________________________	Dated:________________________
______________________________	______________________________
___________________________	___________________________
Attorney for Husband	Attorney for Wife
Dated:________________________	Dated:________________________

ORDER

BASED UPON the Stipulation of the parties, which has been approved by their counsel,

IT IS HEREBY ORDERED that the terms and conditions of the parties' Stipulation are approved and made an Order of the Court. Each party is ordered to comply with all of the foregoing terms and conditions.

SO ORDERED this _____ day of ________________, 2013.

____
Judge, ______________ Court

DISTRIBUTION:

(Attorney)
MITCHELL & ASSOCIATES
9959 Crosspoint Blvd.
Indianapolis, IN 46256

(Other atty)

Courtesy of Gloria Mitchell, Mitchell Law Group

APPENDIX L

CHILD CUSTODY QUESTIONNAIRE

Please do your best to fill out the Child Custody Questionnaire. All information provided is kept confidential between you and our office.

NAME:

OTHER PARENT'S NAME:

CHILD INFORMATION:

Describe your child. (What is your child's personality? What are your child's likes/dislikes? What kind of activities does s/he like?)

Education/Activities:

For each child:

School Grade

Best subject(s) Worst subject(s)

Who drops child off at school?

Afterschool program Frequency Time Child likes/dislikes?

Who picks child up from school/afterschool program?

Extracurricular activity Frequency Child likes/dislikes?

Extracurricular activity Frequency Child likes/dislikes?

Weekend activity: Frequency Child likes/dislikes?

Weekend activity: Frequency Child likes/dislikes?

Does your child have any special educational needs? Are they being addressed currently?

Child's health:

Any particular ailments or medical problems of your child?

Any regular prescription medication for your child? Frequency?

Any allergies for your child?

Child's doctor or health care provider:

Address/phone number:

Who takes child to this doctor?

Child's counselor, psychiatrist, psychologist, social worker, or therapist:

Address/phone number:

Time period seeing the child:

Who takes/took child to this mental health care provider?

Who met with this mental health care provider?

CUSTODY, VISITATION, AND LIVING ARRANGEMENTS:

Is there a custody/visitation court order?

If yes, describe the arrangement the court has ordered for your child.

If yes, have there been any custody modifications from the *original* order?

Is the court custody order being followed as ordered at this time?

If no, what is happening?

What is the current timesharing (ordered or not ordered) of your child now? Fill in for a four-week period (write in "M" for Mother, and "F" for Father)

Sun.	Mon.	Tues.	Weds.	Thurs.	Fri.	Sat.

Is the current situation working or not working?

Do any third parties (significant others, family members, friends, babysitters) help care for the child?

WHAT ARE YOU ASKING FOR AT THIS TIME?

Legal custody:

Physical custody:

Other: Specify exactly what you are requesting regarding ***custody/visitation*** (When do you want the children in your care? When do you want the other parent to have the children?)

What schedule would you **like** to have? ("M" for Mother, and "F" for Father)

Sun.	Mon.	Tues.	Weds.	Thurs.	Fri.	Sat.

RESIDENCE/RESIDENCE HISTORY:

Situation: Rent/Own?_____ Living w/ Family _____

Type: House Apartment

Number of bedrooms? __ Number of people in household? __

Residents:

Name	Age or D.O.B.	SSN	Relationship

Your previous addresses for the last five years beginning with the most recent:

Address	Date Moved In	Date Moved Out	Other persons Living in home

PARENTING ISSUES:

PHYSICAL HEALTH:

List your physicians or health care providers:

Doctor Name Type of Doctor

Address & Telephone Number

Do you or the other parent have any physical or mental health problems that impair your ability to care for your child?

If yes, please explain.

CRIMINAL HISTORY:

Has either parent been charged, arrested, convicted of a crime, on parole, on probation or otherwise been involved with law enforcement agencies?

If yes, please explain.

Location of incident: Date: Case number (if known):

Result (dismissed/acquitted/convicted):

DRUG AND ALCOHOL USE:

Either parent used illegal drugs in the past?

Type Frequency

Either parent currently use illegal drugs?

Type Frequency

Either parent used alcohol in the past?

Frequency

Either parent currently use alcohol?

Frequency

Either parent taking prescription medication?

Type(s)

Any abuse of the medication?

Either parent tested, assessed, or treated for substance abuse?

If yes, when and where was testing/assessment/treatment?

Was it voluntary or court-ordered?

DOMESTIC VIOLENCE:

Has there been physical abuse/violence between you and the other parent?

If yes, please explain.

Has there been mental/emotional abuse between you and the other parent?

If yes, please explain.

Has either parent filed a Temporary Restraining Order (TRO) against the other?

If yes, explain.

Location of case: Date:

Case number (if known):Result:

Has either parent made police reports regarding the other parent or the children?

If yes, please explain.

Location of incident: Date:

Case number (if known):Result:

MENTAL HEALTH:

Have you ever been diagnosed with emotional or psychological issues?

Has the other parent ever been diagnosed with emotional or psychological issues?

Have you ever been treated for emotional or psychological issues?

Has the other parent ever been treated for emotional or psychological issues?

Either parent receiving medication for emotional or psychological issues?

If "yes" to any of the above, please explain

RELATIONSHIP OF PARENTS:

Your relationship with other parent:

From (date) Until (date) Location of residence

If married, date of marriage:

Reason(s) for breakup/separation:

Your *other* relationships:

Name D.O.B. Time period together

Location of residence

Dating/Married

Reason for breakup/separation

Contact #

Name D.O.B. Time period together

Location of residence

Dating/Married

Reason for breakup/separation

Contact #

The **other parent's** relationships:

Name D.O.B. Time period together

Location of residence

Dating/Married

Reason for breakup/separation

Contact #

Name D.O.B. Time period together

Location of residence

Dating/Married